C0069 85905

D1448337

everyone's
a critic

Also by Julia Bueno

The Brink of Being

everyone's
a critic

how we can learn to
be kind to ourselves

Julia Bueno

virago

VIRAGO

First published in Great Britain in 2022 by Virago Press

1 3 5 7 9 10 8 6 4 2

Copyright © Julia Bueno 2022

The moral right of the author has been asserted.

A CIP catalogue record for this book is available from the British Library.

Hardback ISBN 978-0-349-01459-3
Trade Paperback ISBN 978-0-349-01458-6

Typeset in Minion by M Rules
Printed and bound in Great Britain by
Clays Ltd, Elcograf S.p.A.

Papers used by Virago are from well-managed forests
and other responsible sources.

Virago Press
An imprint of
Little, Brown Book Group
Carmelite House
50 Victoria Embankment
London EC4Y 0DZ

An Hachette UK Company
www.hachette.co.uk

www.virago.co.uk

For Jude and Johan,
my favourite critics

Contents

Author's Note

The eight clients I write about are not real, but composite characters drawn from years of conversations in my consulting room, as well as those with colleagues and friends. While I divulge a few facts about myself, I do not share any information in breach of client confidentiality, nor introduce any detail that is identifiable to any client I may have spoken with. Having said that, you may recognise yourself in aspects of some of the stories simply because of the ubiquity of the habit I relate.

If you have always been criticised, from before you can remember, it becomes more or less impossible to locate yourself in the time or space before the criticism was made: to believe, in other words, that you yourself exist. The criticism is more real than you are: it seems, in fact, to have created you.

RACHEL CUSK,
Second Place

Introduction

It's my own fault, my own fault. Everything's
my own fault. I knew I was parting with reason
because this senseless nagging, that it was my
own fault, kept on in some part of my head that
didn't exist.

Mrs Armitage in
PENELOPE MORTIMER,
The Pumpkin Eater

One particularly cold January morning, many years ago, I
pulled back my bedroom curtains and surveyed the frosty
street beneath my first-floor window. I imagined my newly
installed boiler packing up, and my young boys becoming
dangerously ill because I had failed to protect them from their
freezing-cold home. I then noticed my neighbour as he left
his house, trailing white smoky breath, and quickly chastised
myself for not warning him to take care as he walked to work.
My omission could mean he might slip on an icy pavement
and smash his head, leaving his pregnant wife a widow.

Wrestling my mind back from the potential disasters I

could cause, I spotted a man sitting in a car parked opposite my house. He was writing things down, resting his clipboard on the steering wheel, pen lid between his lips. His presence petrified me: I was convinced that he had been sent to spy on me and was compiling a scathing report of my misdeeds.

That morning, my anxious mind was intent on punishing me for my possible wrongdoings. The man with the clipboard signalled the seriousness of my actions and omissions: I had done something – or many things – so dreadful that the authorities had mandated his surveillance. Maybe I'd failed to return a tax form from a previous year of employment. Or perhaps someone had informed social services that I was an unfit mother.

As I ruminated on my many possible transgressions, all the energy drained from my body and I sat down on the bed to recover my strength and my wits. Criticising myself for my lapses, imagined or otherwise, wasn't new to me – in fact this was a habit that caused me frequent bouts of anxiety – but this particular episode showed how hard my self-critic could bite. It, or *she* really, as it's a part of me, managed to convince me that I was *seriously* bad in an objective, state-endorsed type of way.

No wonder I felt so physically weakened. Self-criticism can provoke overwhelming anxiety and paranoia in so many of us – and can affect our internal world in various ways that are damaging or disastrous to living well. It's a mental habit that we aren't often aware of, but I suspect that if you are reading this book you either know, or have a hunch, that you have it. You may even spot others close to you bashing themselves needlessly, wishing they would stop. It's likely. Self-critics are everywhere, and they have kept me very busy in my job as a psychotherapist for the best part of twenty years.

Self-criticism runs like a golden thread through nearly all the problems that people bring to me. Most of my clients don't initially talk about this habit, though, as they don't even realise they have it – instead self-criticism tends to tuck inside many more familiar experiences of distress, such as anxiety (as mine used to do), depression (where it thrives most obviously perhaps), intimacy and relationship struggles, addictions, eating disorders, overwhelming grief and – often at its most pernicious – self-harm and suicidality. You may not be suffering from any of these mental health issues, but my guess is that you could ease up on how you treat yourself nonetheless. I want this book to inspire you to do so.

I share the stories of eight clients whose lives illustrate some of the key reasons we lose the ability to treat ourselves with fairness, kindness, love and compassion. I don't believe any baby is born worried that the pitch of its cry is annoying, or whether its thighs look fat with a nappy on. But over time, assailed by an array of social, cultural and relational influences, we learn to turn in on ourselves, often without noticing. I want you to think more about how much of this applies to you, because that is the first step to learning to do something differently, and to improving your mental health. We have to notice our inappropriate or harsh criticism before we can learn the healthier practice of measured reflection and to foster a greater internal warmth. We may even learn to give ourselves some praise too. In the epilogue, Further Thinking, I point you in the direction of further reading and thinking about the promising road ahead.

Each story explores one or two common reasons why people might have a harsh self-critic – though of course there are many more than I am able to cover in just one book. I don't mean to give parents a particularly bad rap, but they tend to be a popular topic of conversation in my consulting room, and they come up frequently in these stories. It is well established – not just by Freud and other notable psychotherapists in his wake, but by the growing body of developmental psychology research – that parents have a powerful influence on how we learn to treat ourselves. Despite a parent's flaws, I believe, however, that he or she is doing his or her best – they often have their own self-critic to contend with after all.

Parents aren't my only focus. I also look at childhood bullying; the oppressive perfectionism stemming from our contemporary Western culture; persistent stereotypes and prejudice about gender, race and sexuality; our relentlessly pro-natal society; the eviscerating nature of grief; as well as the negative effects of one type of fundamentalist religious thinking. I show how repeated criticism from the outside tends to percolate into our beliefs about our own self-worth.

My stories also show some of the various ways that self-criticism can manifest as detrimental behaviours, such as by making us: people-pleasers, act selflessly at a heavy cost to our own needs, appear arrogant, exhaust ourselves striving for perfection or avoid positive relationships and opportunities. It's no accident that three of the clients in this book are men and five are women, as more women make it to my consulting room than men. Research suggests that women are more self-critical, but also tend to be more tuned in to their self-loathing, and more able to tolerate the vulnerabilities that this experience brings, so they turn to talking therapy more often. My personal experience hasn't convinced me that men are any less self-critical, I think they hide it more.

It's important to say that self-criticism isn't *just* a learned behaviour, but one that is wired into the human brain as a mechanism to keep us safe from real or imagined fears. But there is also no guarantee that a self-critic will emerge as a response to the influences I highlight. We each have our own store of inherent and learned resilience, we are plugged into variously effective support systems, we contend with differing experiences of health and disease, and we have our own DNA that responds to behaviours and our environment in particular ways. There is much more to learn about why – in the words of the author and psychologist Tara Brach – so many of us are trapped in the 'trance of unworthiness', and much more to learn about how, as a society and as individuals, we can help prevent the trance emerging in the first place.

A self-critic isn't always easy to identify, and I hope to help you work out if and how yours is running the show. As one expertly self-deprecatory client put it to me, self-criticism is 'like the wallpaper in my bedroom – always there, but I can't describe it in any detail'. I know a self-critic is in operation when I hear someone talk about disliking, loathing or (unduly) blaming themselves, or when they describe how they suffer with low confidence, low self-esteem or low self-worth. We use many other words to convey our inner antagonist, although feeling 'not good enough' or 'a failure' is more than enough of a clue for me.

A self-critic can be more obvious to those who hear a harsh version of their own voice berating themselves in their minds. The voice may have favourite phrases to put the boot in after you have apparently failed or made a mistake, and these words may be said out loud: 'you idiot' or 'you twat', or far, far worse. If you hear another person's voice berate you in your mind (rather than a version of your own voice), that isn't technically a *self*-critic (I would call it an inner critic), although this distinction easily blurs when another person's voice merges with our own. My ex-boss's shouting voice is clearly not me, but other nasty voices became mine over time.

I want you to learn more about the self-critic's wily behaviours. There are so many ways we tell, and believe, untrue stories about ourselves that are belittling, deflating, deprecatory, disparaging, derogatory or even viciously attacking: a self-critic is creative, persuasive and cunning. We may denigrate certain aspects of ourselves – such as our appearance or how we perform in the office – or, far more destructively, we can varnish *every* aspect of ourselves with pejorative judgement, making the psychological work to remove it far greater.

Ultimately, self-criticism reflects the quality of relationship we have with ourselves. Of course, there are times that we *do* need to keep ourselves in check, but a kindly self-correction rather than self-criticism makes for improved mental and emotional health. I certainly deserve a telling off when my wit becomes too caustic or, as my family would attest, my temper fires too quickly. If all goes well, I can recognise or agree that I've cocked up, apologise, and move on feeling okay about myself, with an intention not to cock up in the same way again. Mistakes make us human. Acute self-criticism about real or even imagined mistakes can spoil, or even ruin, our lives.

Writing about self-criticism feels timely. Since I started working as a therapist two decades ago, I have noted a rising level of self-attack, and thus low self-worth, amongst my clients.

A constellation of catastrophes – an urgent climate crisis, the shambolic legacies of Brexit and Trump, and a global pandemic – have contributed to a greater awareness of our dissatisfaction with ourselves and the way we lead our lives. For many people I have been talking to, this means realising how they have been striving towards competitive ideals that only set them up to fail, and therefore to feel badly about themselves.

There's a story that has done the rounds in certain meditation circles, which I heard on a retreat years ago. I think it shows up how deeply embedded self-criticism is in our culture – but also that it need not be. Sharon Salzberg, an eminent US Buddhist scholar and teacher, wrote about her visit to a conference in India in 1990. Speaking with the Dalai Lama, she asked, 'Your Holiness, what do you think about self-hatred?'

He looked confused. 'What's that?' he asked.

A very wise man was struggling with the idea that a human being could feel so badly towards themselves. When Sharon described how her own self-criticism had caused her great distress as a young adult, the Dalai Lama asked, 'How could you think of yourself this way?' Perhaps he was being deliberatively provocative, knowing only too well of how prevalent self-hatred was in the culture he was forced to flee to, but three decades later his question is even more relevant.

Will Storr fluently unpacks why we are ill at ease with ourselves in his book *Selfie: How the West Became Self-Obsessed*. He examines our relentless search for meaning in a world that has become atomised by neoliberal economics. He charts how we have stripped away state welfare provision while focusing on deregulation and the free market. This ultimately pits us against ourselves and pushes us away from each other. The self-obsession he interrogates is a depleting, self-deluding one, resting on attempts at success that ultimately feed dissatisfaction. We are encouraged to win, achieve, succeed and gain, largely via consumption. And because we have lost our sense of connection with each other, we are thrown back on ourselves, and left to strive alone to prove our worth.

Storr describes the ideal that we are encouraged to aspire to as an 'extroverted, slim, beautiful, individualistic, optimistic, hard-working, socially aware yet high-self-esteeming global citizen with entrepreneurial guile and a selfie camera'. I would add more qualities to this list: wealthy, well-travelled, nutrition-conscious, youthful, maternal/paternal and eco-conscious. These paragons are omnipresent – and normalised – in our parallel virtual worlds, and the dangerously distorting social media platforms operating in them.

The pressures to prove ourselves also make us more prone to egregious otherings. As a white, privileged, cis-gender woman, misogyny is the type of hatred that I have the most personal – and degrading – experience of, but I listen in despair to the prejudice clients describe experiencing because they are people of colour, have a disability or a neuro-difference, are homosexual, or are non-cis gendered. I also talk to people denigrated because of their religion or class. It's hard to feel good about yourself when you are being repeatedly told that you *aren't* good, or worse, when you are treated with utter contempt.

In among our lonesome striving towards an impossible ideal, I also see a potentially destructive demand to be mentally and emotionally well: the wellness industry has created another stick for us to beat ourselves with. I'm all for any lifestyle plan, baroque something-free diet, natural or synthetic drug, meditation practice, sacred mantra or app that alleviates human suffering. But I do worry that the overwhelming proliferation of means to arrive at a notional nirvana stack up to convey the idea that we aren't doing well if we don't enlist them. Although increasing numbers of people seem to be engaging help for their suffering, which is a good thing, many arrive at my door reprimanding themselves for being there in the first place. They feel they have failed if their efforts at self-help haven't worked.

This double whammy of self-criticism – criticising your self-critic – is more prone to happen in a culture that emphasises striving, happiness and wellness like we do. Clients have often reported thoughts to me along the lines of 'I know I shouldn't be so unhappy, it's ridiculous. I have a good job, lots of friends, I do loads of yoga and breathing exercises'. Such thinking leaves little room for the counter-intuitive, more compassionate and frankly more useful practice of acceptance that we are okay as we are, warts and all – just as the Dalai Lama alluded to in his response to Sharon Salzberg.

I certainly don't want to contribute to this double whammy by my emphasis, in this book, on our need to identify, challenge and safely separate from our self-critic. But I do want to inspire a greater awareness in you, so that – at the very least – you can ask yourself why it is that you may treat yourself far worse than you may do your friend, or indeed even a total stranger. My stories show how this has been possible for many of my clients, which means it could be possible for you too.

Chapter One

Early Imprints

Self-criticism, when it isn't useful in the way any self-correcting approach can be, is self-hypnosis. It is judgement as spell, or curse, not as conversation; it is an order, not a negotiation; it is dogma, not overinterpretation.

ADAM PHILLIPS,
'Against Self-Criticism'

Within seconds of opening the door to Charlotte, I knew that she wouldn't want to risk my not liking her. She arrived exactly on time, wiped her feet a few too many times on the mat, and silently waited for me to usher her into my consulting room, and then again, for me to offer her a seat. She assured me that she had already transferred my fee to my bank account, and then carefully tucked her neatly folded coat by her feet as she perched on the edge of the chair.

I knew very little of Charlotte's distress at this stage. Her concise, and polite, email asking to meet with me gave nothing away. Wanting to gauge her experience of being in the room with someone like me, I asked her if she had ever had therapy before, guessing, correctly, that her answer would be no. Without any clues as to how to begin my work with her, I asked her how best I could be of help.

'Generally I'm okay. I've got a good job, lots of friends and a great boyfriend. In many areas of my life I'd say I'm confident. But I keep getting derailed by an immense fear that I've done something terribly wrong. I can feel like I've been an idiot about something, and then I become completely consumed by the idea. Dave – my boyfriend – suggested I get professional help because he can only do so much listening and reassuring. I hate to burden him too, it's so unfair for him to have to talk me down from the edge over and again.'

Sometimes when I meet a client for the first time, it takes a while to understand what brought them to me. It's not always easy to describe our troubles in words, especially if they haven't been articulated out loud before. Also, they may be shrouded in embarrassment, or, even worse, a sickening shame that can lead to silence or a wish to explore peripheral, 'easier', issues first. Investigating the heart of a matter can take weeks, months or even years.

Charlotte didn't disguise the story of her distress though: she had the words. She articulated her presenting issue immediately and in such an efficient way that it betrayed a need to keep herself controlled. Her demeanour, from that first moment of meeting, suggested the same. What she told me sounded horrid for her – and, frankly, familiar to me – but she was also telling me that she was coping well regardless. I suspected that I would need to bide my time before she could let her guard down enough to find, and explore, the parts of herself that she might not have such a handle on. Charlotte could talk about her vulnerabilities well, but as with all clients, I needed her to connect with them more instead.

'Can you tell me more about this "gripping fear"? What "terrible wrong" of yours does it involve?'

'It tends to be the same thing each time. I worry that I've really offended someone, even if I have no real evidence to suggest that I have. I can go from feeling absolutely fine one minute to feeling sick the next, all because of something I may have said or done. Or something I think I've said or done – sometimes I can't even be sure. However much I tell myself that I haven't done anything wrong, it doesn't stop me spiralling down the rabbit hole.'

'Can you give me a concrete example of this sudden switch in feeling? Maybe something that is fresh in your memory?'

By looking closely at just one trigger I hoped to find a clue to the puzzle Charlotte presented – why she was fine, and then acutely not. Often, what seems to be a trivial example is a microcosm of a larger, deeper and intractable problem.

Charlotte didn't miss a beat. 'A couple of days ago, I sent an email to one of the partners at work with some feedback on a document she'd asked me to review. I spent ages on it, carefully crafting my response so it sounded constructive and helpful and polite. She usually responds instantly, but she didn't this time – and she still hasn't. Not even a message to say she'd received it. She's responded to a couple of other emails I have sent her since, though. While I know rationally that there could be many reasons for her delay, I've managed to convince myself that I said something awful.'

Charlotte looked calm, and spoke about this with poise, but I could sense that she was anxious nonetheless. Therapists learn to read small tells – a flush on the face or neck, a tightening of the jaw, or repetitive movements made with hands, fingers, legs or feet. Despite her composure, I noticed a vacancy in her eyes that hinted at a mind that was occupied by unexpressed thoughts. I guessed her mind had raced off into myriad disasters, each of which Charlotte was convinced she was responsible for.

Expert worriers like Charlotte can convey a blissful ease in the world, at odds with a visceral turmoil lurking beneath. It's a trick I learnt too, and although I don't need to rely on it as I did in the past, it can sometimes come in useful in my consulting room when I'm thrown – such as when a client declares an immediate suicidal intention, or directly challenges my worth.

'What is it that you think could be so terrible in this review you sent to your colleague?'

'Maybe I've offended her by being too arrogant with my comments, or I misunderstood the document so completely that she now thinks I'm an idiot. I must have read the email I sent to her about ten times, poring over every single word to work out where I got it wrong. I have also checked so many times that it *has* been sent, just in case it wasn't and she didn't receive it, which would be such a relief.'

'Would you like to show this email to me now? Maybe I could see what I think about the comments you made?'

In saying this, I wasn't really sure that I did want to read the email, but I wanted to check out the reality of it versus how threatening it had become in Charlotte's mind.

'I actually feel sick at the thought of it – my stomach jumped as you asked me that. I'd dread you reading it.'

Charlotte's imagination had thrown her into a state of anxiety that she was doing well to control. This differs from nerves, stress or fleeting worries. Anxiety provokes our brain's threat system, which tells our body to prepare to fight or freeze or flee from the real or imagined threat we face. Its physical symptoms can be mild to debilitating; feeling sick is one common expression, but we can also feel hot, sweaty, jittery, short of breath, suffer headaches or stomach pains, or clench or grind our jaws. At worst we can vomit or, literally rather than metaphorically, shit ourselves.

Anxiety can float around us, moving between various preoccupations, whack-a-mole style. So it could latch on to a performance at work, and then being late for an event. But it can also have more predictable and consistent triggers – heights or spaces, trains or planes, relationships, health or death. But when anxiety seeps into the space between ourselves and another, as Charlotte described, it will always involve a fear of what the other thinks about us. We are very good at imagining judgements by others, especially pejorative ones that cause our status to slip.

'It sounds like you fear *my* judgement if I read the email as well.'

'I guess so, yes.'

'But what if you have – albeit inadvertently – come across as arrogant or idiotic to your colleague? What would happen in this thought experiment?'

Charlotte paused, briefly stumped. 'I don't know the answer to that. Maybe she'll worry about my performance more generally, or she'll talk about how crap I am to others in the team, or she'll just think far less of me.'

'Being talked about, or thought less of, shouldn't make you feel as dreadful as you describe, surely? It sounds to me that a part of you *feels* something much worse than that is going to happen to you. Something really serious, or cata-strophic even.'

'When you put it like that, I can see what you mean. It does feel so much worse than it should.'

'I wonder if deep down you fear being rejected by every-one at work?'

Charlotte nodded her head slowly. 'Maybe. Let me think about that.'

I said this because the type of self-criticism Charlotte described is often bound up with a fear of rejection from others. We are hardwired to rely upon our caregivers and then our social group for survival, but also for our general emotional thriving. As hunter-gatherers we would die from starvation or attack if left to our own devices, while these days it's more likely to be loneliness that kills us.

From just our first meeting I couldn't know how Charlotte would respond to therapy with me, but I was struck by how vicious her self-critic had become. I was also wary of her obvious need to be of little bother to me – to be what we call in the trade a 'good client'. Neither observation made me optimistic: therapy works best when we can allow ourselves to fall apart, and then allow ourselves to mend again with another person by our side.

I was particularly curious about what, exactly, Charlotte's self-critic told her and so when we met again I wanted to understand better why it homed in on the idea of being 'an idiot' or the cause of someone's immense ire. It felt quite spe-cific to me. Sure enough, there were plenty of other examples Charlotte gave me, of times when she felt similarly assailed by a fear of catastrophic failure.

'It's always something silly, really. If someone ignores a question that I ask in a group conversation, in my mind it won't ever be because they didn't hear it, it'll be because what I said was wrong or offensive. A little thing can trigger a cascade of worry that I've done something terrible – and I guess you were right about feeling "rejectable". Then I'll do my own head in going over and over things, berating myself endlessly.'

As we got to know each other, we worked on soothing the physical symptoms Charlotte's repetitive anxious and self-critical thoughts would bring – a racing heart, a tightening of her chest, trouble sleeping and a general jangly feeling. Talking therapy doesn't do its job if it doesn't attend to our bodies too. I didn't see any of her symptoms in my consulting room, though, as she preferred to describe them to me instead: being vulnerable with me in the room ran counter to her self-contained repertoire.

We would meet on a Saturday morning, after her long working week as a junior architect with very demanding colleagues, and even more demanding clients. Architecture is a profession I have learned about from my consulting room, with many students making their way to me in the midst of their gruelling, astonishingly time-consuming training. A few weeks into our meetings, Charlotte arrived much as she had the first time we met: soaked in a sense that she'd done something terribly wrong – yet again. As she spoke, I found myself wanting to shut my eyes.

Many therapists don't just rely on what we see and hear, but also on what we *feel* when we are with our clients – or even what imagery pops up in our minds. These feelings or images could well be ours, provoked by the story we are immersed in, but they could also be our clients', unconsciously transmitted by them and sensed by us from across the room. This magical-sounding experience gives us clues to feelings that may be buried deep in our clients. But it relies on us knowing which feelings are ours and which are out of place or unfamiliar.

When disavowed feelings from a client are unconsciously transmitted (or 'transferred') to the therapist in this way, it's described as countertransference. This process is especially likely when a client can't – or won't – feel their emotions, perhaps because of shame, or because denying their existence protects them from pain. The more widely known idea of transference refers to the unconscious process by which a client replays earlier relationships onto the therapist – a foundational idea of the type of therapy that Freud pioneered with his patients on the couch.

While I listened to Charlotte's story of her self-attack, I felt many of my muscles constrict, which was usual for me – this was my body responding to my wishes for Charlotte of 'No! Don't say that to yourself!' But wanting to shut my eyes was an unfamiliar instinct, something I rarely felt in my consulting room, and this felt important to note.

Charlotte began to tell me about this most recent incident that had left her mired in self-criticism. 'Last night we all went out after work for a colleague's birthday. The partner who hadn't replied to my email was there. I drank far too much and too quickly – Dutch courage – and asked her about it. Needless to say, she had missed it and was very apologetic, she was lovely! She even thanked me for all my good work and promised to check her emails again over the weekend. It was such a relief I drank even more to celebrate.'

Charlotte paused, and poured herself some water with a shaky hand.

'I'm convinced that I made a prat of myself after that and offended someone.'

Charlotte didn't often let her guard down, but alcohol can do this for us very efficiently, as well as giving us a ready and reliable buffer against feelings we'd prefer not to square up to. So many of us depend upon a drink to rub the edges off social anxiety, or just to unwind quickly. Charlotte had experienced a double hangover – the alcohol one and the self-critical one. Or, as some say, 'hangxiety'.

'By the time I got home I had already gone through every conversation I could remember and had sent texts to everyone I had numbers for to apologise if I had offended them. Even though I was drunk I couldn't sleep for ages – my mind was whirring around.'

'No wonder you were kept awake. It sounds like your critical voice was doing a good job of that.'

I could easily imagine the more gregarious Charlotte in the bar, as opposed to the intense young woman in the room with me each Saturday morning. As we spent more time together I'd glimpsed other parts of her personality creeping into our conversations and enjoyed her charm and quick-wittedness. But my fond sense of her was diametrically opposed to her own impressions and the selected memories she brought to me. Hearing her talk through this vortex of self-reprimand drained me in moments – a mere taste of how exhausting her inner world could be.

'I really want to know *why* this punishing mental state of yours keeps taking over. It's a corrupted piece of software that gets activated time and again. Can you remember the first

time that you felt this sickening horror of getting something
so drastically wrong? Go with the first thing that leaps to
mind – it doesn't matter if it doesn't seem to fit.'

Something swept over Charlotte's face, and her voice
changed register.

'Well, my father was good to us in many ways, and I know
he loves us, but he has a terrible temper. He had a tough
time as a child. He doesn't talk about it, but his mother left
him and his brother when they were very young. Unusually
for those days, he was raised by his father, and a number of
nannies. I think this abandonment screwed him up. It made
him insecure.'

'And what does this story of your dad have to do with you
and your beliefs about yourself?'

'Well, he'd point out that I'd get things wrong a lot.'

Charlotte clearly felt disloyal associating her spontaneous
memory of her father with the state of terror she often found
herself in. Giving me some context of his inadequacies – by
telling me of his own childhood wounds – was a powerful
communication to me to go easy on him. Therapy has a reputation for parent-bashing, and it seemed that Charlotte was
pre-empting this. I believe that parents do the best they can
in their particular circumstances, however dire their efforts
may turn out to be. It's how we receive, and make sense of,
these efforts that matters far more. Charlotte shifted a little
in her seat.

'Can you tell me more about your father's terrible temper?'

'Well, he is generally calm – he's a cardiologist, so I guess
he has to be. But he can have explosive outbursts. They were
mainly targeted at my mother, sometimes at my brother, and
occasionally at me. I somehow avoided most of them.'

'How explosive is explosive?'

Charlotte looked at her feet as she continued.

'He'd shout and sometimes destroy things, and sometimes hit my mother – never in front of us though. It would happen behind closed doors. But we could hear everything, of course.'

'How terrifying for you.'

I felt a sinking feeling as she described her father's worst behaviours, and this felt like the shame of a young child to me. No one wants a parent who behaves badly, let alone violently, nor one who harms another parent. Growing up, we desperately want our parents to be consistent and perhaps like others that we know and see in action – other friends' parents, those in books, films, or in our imagination.

'The thing that still bothers me now is that when he did explode, he would always blame someone else for whatever it was he was livid about. He was, and is, incapable of taking responsibility for his rage.'

'I'm curious about that. Because if we don't take responsibility, we'll find someone else to do so instead. Can you tell me about a time that *you* were in the firing line? It may square with this lingering idea that you can cause so much disruption or upset.'

Charlotte took a breath to anchor a barely perceptible unsteadiness. There was a story on her mind already.

'He collects rare books and kept them in his study – we called it 'the library'. No one was allowed in there without him, in case they touched a book. He had special gloves folded up in a case that he'd put on before handling a book, and occasionally he'd let me or my brother try them on and choose a book to look at. One Saturday morning he called me into his study to show me his latest acquisition – a book about

Roman architecture. I was studying the Romans at school and he was excited to show me. I must have been around eight.

'I remember also being excited to be in the library and happy that he'd remembered that I loved drawing Roman villas. I loved drawing all sorts of houses and buildings; perhaps that's unsurprising now. He was sitting in his desk chair with the book on his lap and I stood beside him and he let me turn the tissue guards in between each page, while he turned the precious page itself.

'Somehow his arm on the other side of me knocked a mug of steaming hot water and lemon all over his desk, and lots dripped onto the book. He was incandescent. He threw the book on the floor, grabbed my shoulders and threw me out of the room while shouting at me for what I had done. I fell onto the landing outside.'

I've heard many anecdotes of people behaving unfairly and irrationally, along with too many stories of unbelievable cruelty inflicted on others, but my incredulity at what Charlotte had told me was genuine. I also thought I'd made sense of wanting to shut my eyes in an earlier session – Charlotte may have done this as she was thrown out of the room.

'Wow! So a catastrophe happened in your father's world and his young daughter was the cause, all because she wanted a moment of his time.'

Charlotte briefly met my gaze.

'When you put it like that, it does seem unfair, doesn't it?'

I learned during subsequent meetings with Charlotte that her father blamed her for a whole lot more than damaging a valuable book. There was always a reasonable chance that she was the cause of her father's filthy moods – a slimmer one than her mother or brother, but nonetheless it was an ever-present threat, orbiting the three of them. Although the prompts were often surprising to Charlotte, one predictable source of contempt was not giving her father enough attention at the rare times he was around, or the right quality of attention.

'He could suddenly change from being friendly and warm – he could really make me laugh – to sulking if I didn't find a joke funny, or if I didn't want to do something with him. A sulk was almost always a precursor to rage: he'd simmer and simmer – sometimes for hours, sometimes for days. We'd be walking on eggshells while we waited for the inevitable eruption.'

If we grow up with an unpredictable parent, we may learn to become finely attuned to his or her moods. This hypervigilance is a survival strategy, allowing us to get out of the way of danger, to protect a sibling or another parent, or to work hard to make things better – such as bringing the parent back to good humour, or at least back to a safer mood. We need our caregivers on side as, unlike most other mammals, we can't do without them for a very, very long time.

Charlotte named this hypervigilance her 'Spidey sense'. Her boyfriend Dave was alarmed at how accurately she could read his and other people's moods – detecting the subtlest shifts in emotional temperature during conversations, even without anyone talking. Charlotte had always been tuned in to her father's moods and his presence also loomed large in his absence, which was often, because of his demanding work schedule.

'On the rare occasions he returned from work before we were asleep, my brother and I could tell what mood he was in by the way he turned his key in the front door – he really could do it angrily. If all was well, we'd hang around to talk to him and we would get a hug, and maybe even a tickle. I remember the joy – and relief – of being thrown up in the air when I was very little. But on a bad day, my brother would disappear to his room and I'd try to make Dad happier.'

Charlotte took responsibility for keeping her father happy at an inappropriately young age – and also inappropriately full stop. No child should have the job of looking after a parent's emotional welfare. Through our conversations about this burden, Charlotte started to see the link between her early efforts to placate her father and her ongoing efforts in adulthood to people-please. She also started to connect this to her internalised belief that she wasn't good enough: her self-critic had been fuelled by her father's rage. If someone had spotted Charlotte's burden early on and taken it away, perhaps her self-critic's wings would have been clipped.

The more we spoke, the more Charlotte realised that her drive to please fuelled most of her interactions with other people: bus drivers, her hairdresser, anyone on the street walking towards her, and certainly her big pool of friends. She worked hard to keep conversations going, to ensure others were entertained or at ease, and to pre-empt others' wishes. As we discussed this habit, she became better able to spot it in her actions. One week she began a session with a proud admission.

'You'll be really pleased with me! It was a friend's birthday yesterday and I sent her a message, as well as a present that she should have received on the day. I didn't hear anything from her but rather than thinking I'd got the present completely wrong and insulted her, I was able to pause and think of other possibilities. It was a real relief to be able to see my mind punishing me, and then to re-route it. Fingers crossed I can do it again.'

I had also been a person for Charlotte to please, which is why she had never been a moment late and had kept up her weekly bank transfer of my fee in advance. I don't ask to be paid before a session, and I read her over-efficiency as a means to ensure that she wouldn't let me down by forgetting (as, boringly, some clients do). She never challenged anything I said, but politely corrected me if I got things wrong. And I often sensed her swallowing back a swear-word, in case my feathers were ruffled.

Being a people-pleaser isn't all bad, of course. It can be useful in many circumstances, and probably essential in Charlotte's work in a busy architectural practice with demanding clients and colleagues. It had been in overdrive for far too long, though, so she tirelessly tried to manage the feelings, needs and desires of others at the cost of deciphering what she truly felt, needed or desired. She had come to believe that if she hadn't cared enough about others, she deserved criticism: just as her father conveyed disdain if she didn't care enough about him. But Charlotte's excited report of her 're-routing' was promising.

While Charlotte, as a child, was learning to supervise and manage her father's emotional world, she was also developing a belief that she provoked his bad moods and rages, and therefore that she must be fundamentally flawed. Her father also made it clear that she, along with her brother and mother, were the cause of his ceaseless drive to work all hours at the hospital. Even his workaholism wasn't his fault.

'Dad earned more and more money as we grew up. Our

cars were replaced by other new and expensive cars, and our family home grew in size as we moved to posher and posher areas. Mum started to wear designer jewellery and clothes, and our brief summer holiday became longer and more luxurious.'

Her father's craving for more letters after his name, and more money, meant that he pushed himself through repeated long shifts, little sleep and a near constant level of high stress. Charlotte could now see that the lifestyle he pursued reflected a search for affirmation from a world obsessed with wealth and status. There was a more personal angle too. His mother, who had abandoned him but kept in touch, was a glamorous and socially aspirational woman who had signalled her approval of him through complimenting his material achievements. It was easy to see his striving for a lost maternal love.

Charlotte's father's quest to succeed through professional promotion and material goods was a fragile means to inflate his own shaky self-esteem. It was clear to me that he battled with his own self-critic. Relying on external markers to shore ourselves up can only work as a sticking-plaster, destined to peel off before long – and when it did peel off, his family buffered the inevitable crash in pride.

'He chose a stressful life cycle that meant working hard to earn more to buy more stuff and then make more financial commitments. But the cycle became our fault, and I'd feel criticised. He'd often lash out at us for our unreasonable demands on him. But I didn't ask to go to a private school at five years old, nor to live in a posh area. I remember being really confused when he'd shout at us for wanting so much, when I knew that I didn't want anything really. I just wanted him to be the loving and kind father he could be.'

Looking at Charlotte's father with her through the lens of his obvious narcissistic wounds helped to deepen her compassion for him and for herself, and my own compassion towards him. The more we spoke, the better Charlotte became at realising that her habitual self-recriminations were the result of her childhood. It also didn't surprise me to learn that doing well at school had provided Charlotte with ready currency to buy her father's kindlier attentions; being top of the class guaranteed praise.

'He pegged his pride in me on results: perfect spelling tests, then A-stars, then first class degrees. Coming top mattered most, and he'd always ask if someone beat me. He wasn't interested in anything I did outside the classroom. Even now it's the same – I've run marathons, I've set up a charity and I even cook really well. He's not the slightest bit interested in any of those things.'

Charlotte also began to realise the irony of the life she had chosen: she too had become a workaholic and drove herself to achieve.

'Sometimes I worry that I'm turning into Dad. I don't spend enough time with Dave and I can't remember the last time I cooked for him.'

It was true that Charlotte shared similarities with her father although his motivation to achieve emerged from a desperate desire to show the world how successful he was, and hers came from a fear of failure in other people's eyes. I've lost count of the number of clients who have told me of their fear of repeating the behaviours of a parent they clashed with – it's a common reason for seeking therapy. But I knew that Charlotte would not turn into her father, because she was recognising and talking about the pain his criticism had created.

'One big difference between you and your father, Charlotte, is that you have reached out to me, and you are now working hard to recognise and investigate your distress and think about why it's there in the first place. You aren't leaving it to sabotage your life, and you are already making progress.'

In linking her tenacious, and warped, belief that she was deeply flawed, to her relationship with her father, Charlotte was increasingly able to prise herself away from its grip. She realised that this link had been the genesis of her self-attacks. As we continued our work together, I heard more anecdotes of 'mini-wins' against her self-critic, and reflections upon her reflex to please others in a bid to keep herself feeling okay.

Most of our conversations about Charlotte's past revolved around how she, and sometimes her brother, felt about her father, and I'd often wonder out loud about her mother – she was rarely referred to, and her lack of presence in Charlotte's stories seemed significant. Charlotte wouldn't take the bait. After a couple of months of meeting, I began one of our sessions with my curiosity about her.

'I have no sense of where your mother is when we talk about your earlier life. I wonder why that is?'

'I honestly don't know where she was most of the time. She is, and was, rather ghostlike. She never seemed very happy or interested in us, so we were pretty much left to our own devices from a very early age.'

It turned out that Charlotte had few childhood memories of her mother, even though she had never worked outside the home. Growing up, her mother had often been in bed, 'resting', and from a young age Charlotte and her brother were cooking for themselves in the evenings, while their mother waited for their father to return. She would then prepare a meal for the two of them, although she barely ate herself. I suggested that her mother suffered from depression.

'I've thought about that too, and my brother agrees. Especially after we were born. She has mentioned more than once how tough it was and how she had no help from family. Reading between the lines, I think she was really unwell.'

Thanks to the pioneering work of the child psychiatrist and psychoanalyst John Bowlby and psychologist Mary Ainsworth in the mid twentieth century, and ongoing research since then, we know how we are all hardwired into an 'attachment system' at birth, and what this means for our healthy emotional development. We leave the womb primed to connect with others, and the bonds we forge with our care-givers shape the landscape of our internal world, including the way we relate to other people, as well as ourselves.

If all goes well enough, and our caregivers are sensitive and responsive to our feelings, we are likely to feel secure in the world and therefore trust ourselves and others enough to flourish with relative ease. Donald Winnicott, an English paediatrician and psychoanalyst, emphasised that mothering need not be perfect – the 'good enough mother' would do just fine. But if good enough can't happen, such as when a mother becomes depressed and isn't supported, she may not be able to tune in to her baby in the way that he or she needs.

Depression brings dreadful symptoms of low mood, exhaustion, a lack of self-worth and a mental preoccupation that can corrupt the best of intentions to care for a child. Neither Charlotte nor I knew the real truth about her early months and years, so we only spoke in speculative terms. But she was on far surer ground when it came to describing how her mother made, and makes, her *feel* – which was, roughly, not lovable enough.

'My brother and I always had the sense Mum wanted to be left alone, so we learned to keep our distance. He spent loads of time playing outside in the street with friends or kicking a ball against the wall in our back garden. I'd be inside, often alone, absorbed in a rich world of make-believe. As I said before, I also remember drawing houses a lot. Not far from what I do now, I guess!'

It was this brilliant imagination forged during her childhood that could now, as an adult, conjure up stories that led to intense self-criticism. She was eager to tell me of another sign of her progress. At work that week, a client had called up to chase draft plans, ahead of the agreed date of completion. Rather than immediately apologising and then lacerating herself for doing something wrong, she paused and gently pushed back. This hinted at a decoupling from her ready self-critic.

A couple of weeks after this session, an opportunity arose for one of Charlotte's problematic moments to come alive in the consulting room. It's always fruitful for a client to bring their struggles into their relationship with me. For example, if they are angry with me for letting them down, this allows me direct entry to their experience of feeling let down by others. There have been rare times when I've grabbed such opportunities, such as being provocative with a client fearful of conflict, but I prefer not to manipulate, and I hope for an authentic opportunity to emerge instead. So I was very grateful when that happened with Charlotte, as it nudged the progress she had been making even further along.

I was shocked when, one Saturday morning, Charlotte didn't show up, and even more so when she didn't respond to my message of concern. If she had arrived late I'd have been really surprised, but a no-show was unthinkable, given how reliable – and eager not to disappoint – she was. While I hoped that she had overslept, or as unlikely as it seemed, forgotten, it also crossed my mind that something terrible had happened to her. She had been in increasingly good spirits in recent weeks and had been able to reflect more and more upon how she was making valuable strides in managing her instincts to berate herself at every turn.

When the doorbell did ring, nearly half an hour late and more insistently than usual, I opened the door to a torrent of apologies and excuses. Having left the office in the early hours of the morning after final preparations for an important project, Charlotte *had* overslept. Barely catching her breath, she implored me not to be angry. I couldn't have felt less angry if I tried.

'Dave's away, as otherwise he would have woken me up. I threw myself out of bed but couldn't find my phone anywhere so I couldn't message you. I then missed the bus and ended up walking and running here. I can't tell you how sorry I am!'

Once her unnecessary and plentiful pleas had abated, we didn't have much time left of our session.

'These things happen to the best of us, Charlotte. I'm just glad that you are here, and that you are safe and well.'

'But I feel absolutely terrible! You must have thought I was so rude. Being so late, but also not even bothering to let you know. You have better things to do than wait around for me.'

'I don't think you are capable of being rude. But I was

worried, as I know how reliable you are. And these fifty minutes are yours – I don't have anything else to do but be here for you.'

Charlotte looked away, as she usually did when I spoke of any tender feelings that I had for her.

'But sitting with you here now, feeling the force of your self-recrimination, does make me wonder if it feels for you like it did all those years ago, when you were often shamed into thinking you had caused your father's tremendous fury?'

Charlotte, still looking away, said nothing for a moment.

'Yes, I think it does.'

'I feel a crushing weight of sadness that you feel that way now, and that you felt that way so often as a child. What do you make of that?'

I wasn't lying, or exaggerating for effect. Because I was with her distress in the room, rather than thinking about it as a past event, my response was stronger than ever before. I felt a pressure in my chest as I pictured her younger, baffled self, fearful of causing a disaster and in desperate need of reassurance and care. I noticed how I wanted to shut my eyes tight again.

'I guess I also feel sad for her too. But just a little.'

Our brief time was up, and Charlotte stood to leave. She had never let herself take up more time than she was allocated, and I wasn't going to push this boundary after the difficult revelation she had made. Hearing these few words – almost grudgingly admitted but sincerely felt – gave me hope. Charlotte's sadness for her younger self could be a foundational feeling for her to develop more kindness towards, and compassion for, what she went through, and what she had missed out on. In turn, this could dampen her impulse to punish herself so often.

When we met again the following week, I didn't let Charlotte begin the session as I usually would. I was sure that she would be reluctant to return to the moment of vulnerability that had emerged before we'd said goodbye last time. If we didn't revisit this, I knew she would swerve to talk about safer topics, such as work or friends or her annoying landlady. So I picked up where we'd left off, with the hope she could reconnect with how the there and then could intrude on the here and now.

'Yes. I have thought a lot about what happened. I went home and cried – I can't remember the last time I cried! I felt really raw when I got home.'

I hadn't ever seen Charlotte cry, and it didn't surprise me to hear that she rarely did so, knowing how self-reliant she was. She was more comfortable looking after herself and others than being looked after, having learned to do so at an early age.

'I know we have talked about my childhood and how it bears such an influence on my anxieties, but it feels a little bit different now. I don't just understand it intellectually, but it makes more sense on an emotional level – it was such a release to feel sad about the younger me, and I know I have to do more of that.'

More often than not, working out the psychological maths of what is happening with my clients is just the starting point for further therapy together. Learning what, and how, to feel about the answers is the beginning of, often, much harder work. Charlotte's sadness for her younger self was a step towards the broader compassion she needed to develop for all of her selves – younger and contemporary.

However, she wanted to end our sessions soon after, as she felt equipped with a far greater resilience against her self-persecution. In some ways, despite our many weeks of meeting, Charlotte was just beginning her therapy, but that doesn't always have to take place in the consulting room. She was keen to practise what she had learned about her self-critic out there in her world, among the inevitable triggers for its release. I knew that she was far better able to interrupt the spirals of shame she had initially shared with me; she wanted to continue her psychological work on her own.

About a year later, Charlotte emailed me to tell me that she had moved to a rare part-time position in another architecture practice, so that she could devote more time to the charity she had set up. She and Dave had got engaged, and had bought their first car, which she had reversed into a wall within a week. She had thought of me as she got out of the car to assess the damage.

'As you well know, old me would have felt mortified and idiotic. But even though I knew I was to blame, I laughed at myself in a good way, and was able to quickly move on. Dave didn't think it was quite so funny though!'

I don't often hear from clients and this message was very cheering. Charlotte's anecdote spoke of her increasing ability to be kinder to herself, which had begun when we said goodbye. She was taking on board that her self-critic was often vicious and wrong, and that its erroneous beliefs were embedded in a past she wanted to think about differently.

Chapter Two

Meanies

Yesterday I was clever so I wanted to change the world; today I am wise, so I am changing myself.

I first heard Daniel's voice in a peremptory voicemail telling me that he wanted to sound me out for a brief course of therapy. I was tempted to text him an apology for being too busy to see him, as I didn't like the sound of his bossy tone. Then I reminded myself of the many times I hadn't initially warmed to a client before growing to like them and to care for them, sometimes deeply. It helps to like a client from the start, but it isn't essential; sometimes, not liking a client is a good indicator of their own dislike of themselves. Self-criticism can play out in this paradoxical way.

When I spoke to Daniel over the phone, he was quick to tell me that, as a senior employee of a management consultancy, he was receiving executive coaching to expand his leadership and management skills. In his most recent session, the subject of his private life had come up, and his coach suggested that he could benefit from reflecting on some themes that were beyond the realm of his business performance. The coach – an ex-colleague of mine – had suggested he see me: a coach often hands the baton to a psychotherapist when deeper psychological work is necessary.

The overwhelming majority of clients I meet these days set up an initial face-to-face assessment by email or text, or even WhatsApp or Instagram message, but I understand why someone would want to check me out on the phone before coming to my consulting room. In the past I have also needed to know that a potential therapist sounds, at the very least, kind and open and able to help – or as another wary client once said to me, 'I just want to make sure you don't sound like a complete psycho.'

It seemed that Daniel didn't need to know if I had any warm qualities, or if I was mad or not, but he did need to know that I was clever. He asked a few penetrating questions about my five-year training and the qualifications I'd accrued (no one before or since has asked me what grade I got in my dissertation), before asking me for a summary of my theoretical stance. This is not easy at the best of times. I must have done a good enough job of answering, though, as he agreed to meet for an initial session. I hung up and exhaled, not realising until then how tense I had become while trying to pass his test.

When we met in person for the first time, I struggled to feel affection towards him. Although Daniel told me that he had done plentiful research on psychotherapy, and had read all the content of my website, including my blog posts that talk about my work, I wasn't convinced that he wanted to examine his inner world. He seemed to want a quick fix to his problem, and for me to tell him what the fix was.

'I turned thirty-five last month and I think it's time for me to find someone and settle down. I have a great job, I'm in good health, I'm financially stable and I have just moved into my own flat.'

'You say you *think* you should settle down now. Do you know whether you *want* to?'

I had hoped to create a space for reflection upon this potentially important difference, but Daniel didn't take it up. It was too early to tell if he was distracted by well-hidden nerves at meeting a stranger to talk about his private life, or if he didn't want to work out the difference, or if he couldn't understand what I was driving at. Or something else I couldn't guess. He pressed on.

'Most of my colleagues and friends are married, getting married or having children now. I have yet to find the right person, and it seems right to follow suit.'

'How long have you been single?'

Daniel did pause this time.

'I've never had a significant relationship, if that's what you are getting at. I date a lot of women though.'

'If most people you know are settling down, my guess is that you feel left behind. Or even lonely?'

I wouldn't usually leap in with a guess so early on in a relationship with a client, but I already knew that Daniel would need nudging towards self-reflection. I'd tried a few times when we had spoken on the phone, to no avail. As I suspected it would, my suggestion landed somewhere between us, not quite reaching him: being asked about a feeling was a challenge for someone keen to solve problems with his intellect alone.

'Not really. I work extremely hard and I'm with people

all day.' He remained motionless bar his eyes, which darted everywhere apart from my gaze. 'I'm either talking to clients or members of my team, so I'm far too busy to feel lonely. But now's the time for things to change, because there are evenings and weekends to fill.'

Daniel's rebuff didn't convince me. At this early stage, I relied both on his obvious unease in his body and on my experience of talking to many other expressly sorted people like him, whose apparent confidence turns out to be a defence against actually feeling unsorted. I suspected that he didn't enjoy time alone because he didn't enjoy being with himself, however much he signalled otherwise. I wondered if, buried deep beneath the bluster, there was a part of him undermining his self-worth.

'It sounds like it doesn't feel okay to be on your own any more?'

'It's fine. But as I say, I want a change.'

Daniel spoke with an air of irritation.

'Fine' is a pretty meaningless word when it comes to describing how we feel, and Daniel would use it a lot with me. 'I'm fine' has to be one of the most socially acceptable lies told in the English language, and I often surprise (and probably bore) my friends by replacing it with a truthful response. I inhaled a bit too loudly to steady myself against Daniel's implicit pushback. A hypervigilant client might have spotted this as a prelude to a sigh, but Daniel wasn't one of them. He wasn't interested in what went on between us, instead wanting me to focus on a solution for his single status.

'Can you tell me how I can help you with your quest to meet someone to settle down with?' I asked.

'I meet a lot of women on dates, but very few make it to

a second date and even fewer to a third. In fact, I've never made it beyond three. I wanted your professional opinion as to why that is. Maybe I'm choosing the wrong type of woman to begin with? Or I could be ignoring obvious signs that they aren't right for me?'

'That's an interesting idea that we can think about. But I think it's also worth us considering that you could be playing a role in this pattern. Perhaps we can think about how these women may be responding to *you* as well, as we don't always know what we are like in other people's eyes. If we carry on meeting, I hope to get to know you far better than I can ever know any of the women you meet.'

Therapy is rarely easy, nor is it something I can straightforwardly deliver. I wanted to be clear that I couldn't offer Daniel what he seemed to want. I wasn't going to prescribe him a winning dating formula or be able to say, 'If you choose a woman with these personality traits, all will be well!' Given his obvious resistance to investigating his emotional world, I thought it fair to spell out what lay ahead with me – which would involve his looking inward, and at how he *really* felt about himself.

'If we commit to further sessions together, I will want us to think about how and why you arrived to be the thirty-five-year-old man you are now – the person who succeeds at work, is in great health, has bought a flat, dates lots of women, wants to settle down, but remains single. I'd want to hear about significant events that may or may not have had an impact on you, and how you have learned to respond to your world.'

Daniel shifted ever so slightly, for the first time that I could notice. I knew he'd bristle at my plan. Still working hard to avoid my face, he took in the contents of my room. Over many years, I have filled my space with knick-knacks, paintings and postcards, and hundreds of books that are meaningful to me. I find comfort, and practical use, in having these things near me, and they often prove to be useful discussion points with clients, especially if words don't come easily. But they can also offer a ready distraction from the intensity, and benefits, of eye-to-eye contact.

'I read what you wrote on your website about the benefits of examining the past, but I can tell you now that my life so far has been absolutely fine. Nothing eventful happened growing up. I had a happy childhood, did very well at school and my parents are still together. But you also write that you hope to offer practical help, so I want you to concentrate on that, please. I'm clearly choosing women wrongly, and I need to know how I can improve this.'

I understand the desire of anyone in distress to be fixed fast. But as we've got increasingly used to gratifying our desires instantly, therapy can be burdened by our need for swift resolutions. I often meet clients wanting me to work magic within weeks, and more often than not this kind of urgent request comes from my male clients.

Men still bear a greater social pressure to not be vulnerable, and if they have gone as far as to admit that they are, they tend to want to pull themselves up by their bootstraps with pragmatism, rather than embark on a sensitive enquiry into their emotional world. With Daniel, though, the remarkable distance he put between his problem and his feelings didn't strike me as entirely due to a stereotyped masculinity. Being full of yourself, as Daniel seemed to be, usually means you feel empty deep down inside.

By the end of our first session, my early impressions had

been confirmed: his annoying swagger was a clue to a hidden, uneasy relationship with himself. And I'm habituated to give people the benefit of the doubt, and always to leave open the possibility that vulnerability is tucked behind unlikeability. In order to understand what had happened to make Daniel like this, I needed to be a woman who could get beyond his third date record.

I wouldn't have been surprised if Daniel hadn't returned to see me. I didn't offer what he said he wanted, and I had made it clear that I wanted us to talk about things that he had no interest in. I didn't think that he liked me very much either, not least because of my irritating questions and my sympathy that he didn't want to receive. However, he emailed the next day to confirm his wish to continue meeting, albeit in cool terms and on the basis of a trial. It seemed that I'd do for a while.

When we met for the second time, Daniel quickly steered the conversational focus not towards himself, but in his favour: he indulged in telling me, in some detail, about how clever he was. It's usual for clients to take a few moments at the start of a session to warm up, especially in the early weeks, when we are getting to know each other. In true British style, we often exchange pleasantries about the weather – clients arrive hot or cold, wet or windswept – or maybe we'll refer to some dire news from the world outside. It's not always easy to transition from our accustomed day-to-day conversations to one that is a very different type of exchange, centred entirely around yourself. But this wasn't the case for Daniel.

Although he had come to me for my professional help, and I was clearly a good few years older than him, neither of these facts dissuaded him from emphasising his expertise in a wide variety of topics. He would often start a session, and indeed a sentence, with something like: 'The thing about X . . . ', before telling me, definitively, about X and then rounding up with a resounding, 'And that's the thing about X.' My efforts to divert him from his dull mini-lectures, perhaps by guiding him to reflect on a statement he'd made, or suggesting they were metaphors for his feelings, were often futile.

One time, Daniel told me in great detail about what it was like to be a working mother, on the basis of a conversation he had had with a colleague. Another week he gave me a potted history of a town in Guatemala he had visited on holiday the previous year, along with an inaccurate summary of the country's long-standing political traumas. In a rare leak of self-disclosure, prompted by my intense irritation, I told him that I knew Guatemala well and I gently corrected him on his biggest factual error (I had, in fact, lived in the town he was telling me about for six months in my twenties). He clearly didn't like my modest amendment, as being right kept his self-worth together.

Of course, Daniel couldn't know what I did or did not know about the world; therapists tend to keep their cards close to their chest. This keeps us out of the way and focused on our clients' experiences. Nonetheless, I was bemused by his lack of awareness that I might have some knowledge of what he spoke about. He knew from his early interrogation that I am well educated, and my consulting room and website both suggest that I read a lot and have travelled widely. But acknowledging these aspects of me would have threatened Daniel's desperate need to be the all-knowing one in the room. By keeping me at arm's length with his intellectual prowess, he was fending off any chance of my finding out about and exposing his vulner-abilities – including the possibility that he lacked confidence.

Daniel's relentless inclination to topple me intellectually irritated me, but I also reflected on my growing desire to beat him at his favourite pursuit, of being clever. I enjoyed correcting him about Guatemala. I'm generally seduced by the lure of conversational sparring, as a relic of both my brief career in law and my historical efforts to prove myself worthy against my own self-critic. But I don't often feel *mean* about my opponent, and this was an uncomfortable but important feeling to monitor, precisely because it felt unfamiliar. It was a countertransference and so suggested that Daniel had been treated meanly before.

Daniel attempted to reiterate his superiority by repeat-edly describing his professional successes. He talked about his role as a management consultant in some detail, with semi-frequent nods to the fact that he had been fast-tracked through promotions at a young age. I heard a lot about the long hours demanded of him, the messes made by colleagues that he had to clear up, his frequent meetings with seniors around the globe, as well as the 'brainless' clients he had to please. I wasn't called upon to share any observations, or to probe further into any of this, as Daniel's work life was unproblematic. His executive coaching, as he'd expounded to me, had focused on developing his established skills rather than working on any deficits.

I also learnt about Daniel's shiny academic credentials from distinguished universities, as well as how prestigious his employer was. And I was told, again and again, that he had plenty of money. He consumed ostentatiously: he would carefully fold his suit jacket in such a way that I could not fail to see its label. Even my untrained eye discerned bespoke tailoring. I'd clench my teeth each time he flicked something from it onto my floor.

When we would eventually get around to talking about Daniel's most recent dates, he would name-drop expensive restaurants along with the vintages of bottles of wine he had bought. This verbal tic bored me, but I kept running with the idea that it was a means by which he soothed his low self-worth. However, his bragging about his wealth felt particularly galling after a few weeks of failing to pay me.

'Hearing you talk about your expensive dinner reminds me that my fees remain outstanding. Did you get my reminder?'

Therapists must talk about the payment of their fees upfront, just as they must talk about sex and suicide with frankness and confidence. Early on in my career, I used to prefer to talk about sex and suicide over discussing any issues about the exchange of my services for another's money. My reticence keyed into a lack of conviction in my worth as a therapist, but also into our cultural awkwardness in talking about money generally. I could sense Daniel's discomfort as he responded to me.

'Ah yes! I hadn't forgotten. Thank you for reminding me. I haven't yet paid because I was a little confused. I thought you charged more than you put on your invoice, as I remembered your website stating a higher fee.'

I use a template, so I knew I hadn't made an error, and I said so.

'Ah okay. I'll settle up then. But I'm happy to pay more if you want. Maybe you should charge more than you do?'

Although this could be understood as flattering, I didn't feel that Daniel's suggestion, nor tone, was kind. Rather than telling me that he thought I deserved more remuneration for my work, he was suggesting that my carefully considered fee was questionable. I felt undermined by this and any doubt about him needing to feel superior to me evaporated. His persistent desire to know better was also wearing thin, and it felt to me that instead of doubting my own adequacy and worth, he really doubted his own. I needed to work hard to approach his lively self-critic, hidden under the thick layer of bravado.

While I often felt under scrutiny during our sessions, I forgot for a while that Daniel had begun therapy with me on tentative terms. It's not unusual to have a review after a few weeks of meeting regularly, but it's rare for me to have one set up by a client before work begins, as Daniel had done. When I eventually asked him whether my probationary period was up, he hurriedly assured me that he was happy to continue meeting, waving his hand in a dismissive way.

'I'm glad that you are continuing to see me, Daniel, as I'm still hoping to help you forge a lasting relationship with someone, and we're not there yet.'

This was true, although I knew he wouldn't enjoy this observation about our work together. Looking at us would have required him to think about our relationship, and how he felt about seeing me each week. Turning inwards, towards his feelings about another human being, might have edged too close to how he was actually feeling about himself. Instead, Daniel immediately deviated into a dull discourse about probationary periods at his place of work. But his didactic monologue lacked its usual verve, and I noticed he hadn't gone through his usual procedure of jacket-folding, nor of emptying his pockets of their expensive digital gadgets onto the table between us.

I interrupted him with a raised hand and a slightly raised voice.

'You seem different today. What's up?'

I didn't expect a proper answer to this and was taken aback when I got one.

'Well, I've been thinking quite a bit these past couple of days. The other night I took my team out for drinks after a really long day with a difficult client. It's important to keep the team bonded at times like this, you see. It's rare for Ben – my best assistant – to join us after work, as he has young kids and usually wants to head home.'

Daniel then couldn't resist telling me about the importance of a father figure for children, and of the statistics concerning the gender division of labour in the domestic sphere. As I quietly swallowed his pontificating, I privately noted how remarkable it was that he hadn't mentioned the name of the bar he had been so generous to take his team to, nor the names or prices of the inevitably expensive cocktails he had bought for everyone. I waited, letting his words pass by like tumbleweed, until he returned to what he'd said he'd been thinking about.

'Ben's mother died recently, and he's had some compassionate leave. We've spoken a bit about some developments in a project that he's working on, but I thought I'd check in on him informally over a drink. My coach has suggested I spend a bit more time with my team. As we chatted, the subject of therapy came up because he wanted to ask me for flexibility as his weekly session time had changed.'

Any mention of therapy in a social or work context would

have surprised me twenty years ago, when I first had my own therapy. Back then, the talking cure was shrouded in unhelpful mystery, and often allied with the idea of a psychoanalyst – like Freud – sitting beside a couch, not looking at his or her patient, while dissecting dreams and exploring fantasies of maternal breasts. It was often thought of as a treatment for serious mental ill-health, rather than an appropriate route towards better, and sustained, mental health, as it is now widely regarded. The couch is a rare feature these days too.

'Ben told me how helpful his therapy had been during his mother's illness and that he was still working out a lot of things about his childhood. It was interesting to hear. I ended up telling him that I'd been coming here, and that you wanted me to talk about my past. He was quite persuasive about my doing so. He said he had made sense of many patterns of behaviour he'd felt trapped by.'

It rankled that Daniel needed permission from someone other than me to reflect on his earlier experiences. It seemed as if all my efforts to inspire him to look inwards, and backwards, and beyond himself, had been meaningless, whereas the opinion of someone he wouldn't usually take advice from had made a difference. But as long as a part of him doubted he was good enough, his resistance to connecting with me – and women more generally – would continue. I backed away from noting all of this out loud, as I knew he wasn't ready to hear it.

'Well, I think Ben's on to something. I suggest that we do it. You don't have to start at the beginning, but perhaps start with letting me know more about your life story. All I know is that you had an uneventful but "happy" childhood.'

It was clear that this was a new and uncomfortable trajectory for Daniel, as words did not pour out of him in his usual, often dogged, manner. Nor was I surprised that his first descriptions of his parents focused on their professional lives, rather than their personalities. I didn't expect to hear much about his feelings towards them, or what he thought they felt about each other.

'My father has just retired. He ran the local planning department. My mother started out as a planning assistant after she left school – that's how they met. They were married after about a year together, and she had me soon after, and then my sister Gillian arrived eighteen months after me. Then, when we were both at school, she became a librarian. The library was next door to our primary school.'

Daniel began to tell me in some detail about the Dewey Decimal System, and how it is driven by discipline rather than subject. Ignoring his diversion, I beckoned him back to thoughts of his mother with a hackneyed therapy question, which I knew he'd baulk at.

'What do you remember of your mother growing up?'

I could see how he tried not to roll his eyes.

'Not much. I remember her more when we were at school, as it had close ties with the library. Each week, a class would visit to borrow books. Gillian and I would have to go there after school and wait until her shift finished. There would always be other kids there too, waiting to be picked up – it was a bit like an unofficial after-school club. But we'd sit in the office at the back. I'm not sure why we couldn't sit with the others.'

'What was that like, having a mum so close to you, in the library next door to school?'

Daniel shrugged.

'It was fine.'

But then he gave me a smile that lit up the room, and instantly warmed up my feelings for him. He knew by now that 'fine' was not going to cut the mustard, and that I would press him if he didn't explain further. This felt like an important shift between us.

'Well, it was a library, so part of Mum's job was to keep it quiet, which was difficult with loads of young kids. She got a bit of a reputation at school for being the strict one while her colleague – I'll never forget his name – Mr Kimpton was the fun one and he didn't care so much about noise. He always had a stash of sweets in his drawer that he'd give to kids if they answered his quiz questions correctly. The whole school loved him, and my mother didn't have a chance.'

'That sounds tough. How do you know what the kids thought about your mum?'

Knowing what we can be like when we are young, I guessed he had heard some pretty mean things about her. Daniel was clearly uncomfortable remembering these moments but he thankfully resisted the urge to change the subject. We were still on our maiden voyage into his childhood.

'I wouldn't say it was tough, but it wasn't nice. And some things were said that were pretty unfair.'

'Such as?'

He couldn't tell me, because – I guessed – they were too upsetting to say out loud.

'Well, as I said, just things about her being strict while Mr Kimpton was so nice.'

'No child I know likes to hear bad things said about their parent, even if their parent is obviously bad. And no child I know likes to feel different. It must have been painful for you, and I'm guessing for Gillian as well.'

Daniel shrugged and his eyes drifted to my bookshelf.

'I honestly don't remember being bothered. They just didn't understand Mum was doing her job.'

'Well, I reckon it would have bothered you, even if you can't remember it. And if I'm right, it must have been a difficult subject to talk to your mum about. If all goes well, we can take our worries home with us and unpack them there. But I imagine you wouldn't have wanted her to know what was going on. That would have been difficult.'

Daniel's face softened with another, but much smaller, smile.

'Not really. Because I definitely wouldn't have talked to her!'

'You say that very quickly and emphatically.'

'My mother doesn't talk about anything much at all! Nor my father. We aren't a family of conversation. I make up for everyone on the talking front.'

I had been thinking the very same.

Once we had begun to talk about Daniel's past, our sessions took on a different rhythm. As I became more familiar to him, his body released some of its tension – he looked at me more, let his shoulders slump, and his usually motionless face softened more and more into his wonderful smile. As he gained confidence in finding the words for and then speaking about his experiences (rather than about issues or things), he became more willing to let me ask questions about his life and was less tempted to digress into didactic monologues.

I heard about a childhood home that was not only quiet but also seemed to be emotionally arid.

'Can you tell me more about family life without conversation? What were meals or weekends or holidays like, for example?'

'Mealtimes are easy to remember because we would only talk about the food we were eating. My mother isn't an amazing cook, but she would always make *a lot* of food, and she always fussed over whether we had eaten enough. It was an unspoken rule that Gillian and I would have to finish everything on our plate before leaving the table.'

'And your father?'

'My father is not a man of many words. Mum would talk about the meal, and her work at the library. We'd talk about lessons. He'd be silent.'

'What if you were upset about something? A grazed knee or a spat with a friend or worry about school. Would you talk about that at all?'

Daniel shook his head, and almost laughed at the thought.

'No! We all kept ourselves to ourselves. My parents aren't good at talking about problems, or anything much really. Dad would have sent us to Mum if we were upset. And she would just give us a biscuit or cake and send us on our way. Looking back, I know I faked being upset at times, just to get a treat.'

Cooking for, and feeding, others is not an unusual way to express love and concern. But food can be used to soothe and anaesthetise tricky feelings if we can't bear to suffer our own pain or see it in others. Giving a sobbing child some sweets is tempting for many parents, but it runs the risk of avoiding a more useful discussion about what the upset is about, and how best it can be managed. I wondered if Daniel's mother also used food as an alternative to the words and gestures that she didn't seem to have had at her disposal.

'Do you think your mum used food as a way of showing her love to you?'

Daniel didn't leap to correct me as he might have done

before. The themes of love, feelings, emotions and intimate relationships had been unfamiliar ones for him to explore, but he had become increasingly willing to tolerate them.

'Maybe. She certainly isn't the touchy-feely type. My grandmother, her mother, was the same. She would bake for days before we visited, and we would leave with stacks of Tupperware boxes. I don't remember ever being hugged by her, though, or, come to think of it, seeing her hug Mum.'

While I thought about Daniel being fed so much, I imagined that he might have been overweight. He was proudly trim when I met him and frequently told me about his crack-of-dawn workouts with his celebrity personal trainer, but they seemed to benefit a body he saw in the mirror rather than one he inhabited. Somewhere along the way, he had disconnected his mind from his body, and all the feelings the latter held.

Although I had detected an increasing relaxation in his body in recent weeks, Daniel was still largely a 'mind-taxi', as one punchy colleague described people like him. While being overweight is not an inevitable cause or result of this mind–body disconnection, being unhappily overweight (or indeed underweight) often is. With another client, I might have asked directly if large meals and sugary snacks had led them to put on weight, but I still felt nervous of Daniel's edges, and I wanted to tread carefully.

'If you ate a lot, did this mean you ate more than you needed to?'

He barked back, 'Yes.'

'Were you overweight?'

He made a point of looking at me directly. 'Yes.'

'Enough to be obviously fat?' I got there in the end.

'Yes, I was.'

'And how was that? I know that we can be cruel about differences we spot in each other when we are kids.'

'There were a few unpleasant comments. I wasn't bullied, though, if that's what you are getting at. I had friends, and I didn't really care about nasty things people said about me or my mum. And I wasn't hit or anything like that.'

Most of us want to distance ourselves from the idea of being a bully. But admitting to being a victim can also be shame-inducing as it forces us to confront painful feelings of rejection and humiliation. We tend to think of bullying as intentional, repeated physical or verbal aggression – hitting, slapping, pushing, taunting or making threats – but it can also be far more subtle and nuanced.

Schools in Daniel's day weren't as good as they are now at spotting, and dealing with, bullying – nor did they have to deal with the relatively new phenomenon of cyberbullying. Having said that, many young people still suffer from it. The 2019 Annual Bullying Survey published by the charity Ditch the Label reported that one in five young people (aged twelve to twenty) had been the victim of bullying, with the most citing their appearance as the hook that bullies held on to.

Daniel's emphatic denial sounded synthetic, and his jiggling leg told me more than he was prepared to. As we sat in silence, we both realised that he may not have shrugged off repeated hurtful comments after all, and that a part of him had come to believe his young critics. They had sparked a belief in himself that he wasn't fundamentally okay. Although he had said one thing to me about it, we both knew that he actually meant another. I wouldn't ever get to grips with the full extent of his experience at school, but I strongly suspected it had been cruel.

'I need convincing that you didn't care what others said to you. I know you have a tough skin now, but I'm not so sure you did back then. Especially as you couldn't go home and ask for help.'

Daniel shifted in his seat, and quietly muttered, 'Maybe.'

I pictured him alone in his bedroom after a bad day at school, feeling dreadful about his body and himself, and I noted how differently I felt towards him as compared to when we first met. I had, at long last, met the wounded part of him which had come to believe that he deserved putting down. I thought that if he could also meet this part, with compassion, his chances of intimacy with other people would greatly improve. In other words, if he could face himself he'd be better able to let others do the same.

While our conversations became a bit easier for me over time, they became harder for Daniel. He was willing to think more, and more deeply, about his experiences, but I could see that this was draining, and that he often lacked the vocabulary to describe his internal world. He had spent most of his life talking about topics external to himself, as I knew only too well: economics and politics, fine wine and management consultancy, Guatemala and the Dewey Decimal System.

Daniel had few memories of his younger years, and certainly no happy ones – birthdays, Christmases, holidays had all faded away. Of course, it's reasonable not to remember much from three decades before, but I never quite knew if he was choosing not to share recollections because they were difficult. He described his few friends at primary school as quiet and bookish like him, and he had often read during break to avoid the threats of the playground. One teacher, clearly spotting his introverted ways, had let him help her prepare for lessons and sort books out for the class.

'I loved learning and it's all I wanted to do. I always had a book in my hand. Mum had to get books out of the library storage stacks for me as I had read everything on the shelves. By the end of my time at primary school I was focused on passing the grammar school entrance exam. I was determined to get in.'

'And I bet you did.'

Daniel smiled and I enjoyed the connection between us.

'Was secondary school any better?'

'Not much. I was a hard worker there too, and I just wanted to do well. I kept a fairly low profile and hung out with others like me – the quirky, geeky and unpopular boys. We'd program computers together, enter maths competitions and things like that.'

'Why a low profile?'

'There was a bunch of boys in our year who made life difficult for everyone, but us in particular. I had an operation for a lazy eye and had to wear a patch for a bit. I then had to wear glasses, and this was way before they were cool, and then – *ta-daa!* – I got acne. I had the triple whammy: fat, four-eyed and ugly.'

Here were more clues to Daniel's submerged self-critic. I was taken aback by his open and raw assessment of his teen self, while feeling a pang of sadness for him. By this stage, I had greater faith in his ability to feel more tenderly towards himself. I tried a question.

'Is that how it felt? That you were fat, four-eyed and ugly?'

Daniel jiggled his leg and took more time than usual to respond.

'I was often reminded of one of those three things by other kids, so it was hard not to feel like an outcast. But I knew that I was clever, and that I could beat everyone in the classroom. From the day I arrived at secondary school I thought about the day I would leave – much like I did at primary school. I remember looking at an honours board outside the main hall and setting myself the goal to have my name on it. If I couldn't win as a popular pupil, I was going to win academically.'

He *had* won the competition he set for himself. But he'd spent most of his school years excluded from a tribe, bearing the soul-crushing rejection of the more powerful members. It made perfect sense that he'd kept himself apart from close relationships as an adult, safe from the risk of further ridicule, and it made sense that he'd ended up recriminating himself for being rejectable, without even realising.

During the time we had been working together, Daniel had continued to meet many women – some via dating apps, a few at work events and others through an eye-wateringly expensive dating agency. In our early sessions, we had followed his theory that he was attracting a type of woman who was destined not to appeal to him. But this idea didn't hold water for long. He told me about the trainee landscape gardener, the workaholic lawyer, the free-spirited teacher and the fellow management consultant. They were very different characters, and their photos (he would illustrate his stories with his smartphone to hand) showed wildly different-looking women too.

When we first talked about his dating life, I'd hear a perfunctory report of the evening with little more than the name of the venue, cost of the bill and whether they were planning

to meet up again. I was pretty sure he was letting himself
down with his need to impress by being flashy, opinionated
and, at worst, arrogant. He made it very difficult for anyone –
date or other – to get to know him. Even though it had been
my main job, it had taken me a long while to even begin to
get there.

I wasn't ever quite clear whether Daniel had decided not to
invite them on another date, or whether his date had declined
an invitation, as his pride was often buffering the truth.
Details of how Daniel actually *felt* about the woman he had
met, or what he imagined she had thought about him, were
hard to come by.

'She was fine, but no,' he would say, or 'The Wagyu beef was
perfectly cooked, but our table was too close to the kitchen.'

But as our weekly meetings rolled on, Daniel cautiously
began to open up about his lonely and bullied past, and this
allowed him to tolerate the idea that he wasn't emotionally
invincible after all. I hoped that he would understand how he
had avoided intimacy, and in turn link this avoidance to his
lack of compassion for himself. In time, I enjoyed hearing of
his growing interest in human relationships and emotions,
and what made people tick – his dates included.

It was new to hear him reflect on a colleague's demeanour
at a meeting, or for him to notice his mum's tone of voice
during a dutiful phone call. I also felt less like a treatment-
giver and more like a person he related to, and he surprised
me one week by commenting on my new haircut. Daniel's
reports of his dates became more colourful, and more engaging to hear about, as he talked less about their setting or the
food and more about the person he was with.

'She was captivating. I wish I'd got to know more about

her, but I think she might be very shy.' Or, another time, 'Poor woman has been through so much in her life. It's amazing what she's achieved.'

On my recommendation, he listened to podcasts and read books about human lives – memoirs, biographies, interviews and even therapy case studies. I wanted him to develop his emotional repertoire, and to practise his empathy through thinking about other life stories. I remained convinced that his habitual self-absorption sprang from a painfully wounded part of himself that still feared rejection, rather than from a conscious choice to be selfish.

One week, he proudly told me that he had been moved to tears by a film I'd suggested. It was about a lonely and difficult young boy who is nourished by a relationship with an equally lonely elderly neighbour. Daniel didn't bore me with a monologue about the director; instead, he dwelt on the idea that he had seen an aspect of himself in the little boy and had felt moved. I commented on the film, knowing Daniel would know I was actually referring to him.

'It sounds as if that friendship restored the little boy's belief *in himself* as likeable.'

Daniel smiled, nodded and – I hoped – took a moment to feel warmer towards his own experience as a little boy, when he had no neighbour to help him. While Daniel ventured into the realm of emotions and practised his new skill of self-reflection, it became increasingly clear to us both that his dating disappointments were not due to his choosing the wrong women. And then he met Zoe, and he told me about this date with a look in his eyes that I hadn't seen before.

'I had the best evening – we talked for hours. I walked her home after we ate, it was about five miles, and I ended up telling her about the tough times I'd had at school. She teaches at a secondary school and has a real interest in the mental health of her students, so I knew she'd get it.'

This was the first time he had told anyone apart from me about being bullied, and Zoe was a perfect candidate to listen: she had a pastoral role at her school, but also ran a club at the weekends for children who were anxious about attending school. I guessed that Zoe knew boys like Daniel, as well as kids like those who picked on him.

'To be honest, it felt good to talk to her about it all. And we have an unusual second date: she asked me to help out with some gardening work at her school this weekend. I'm really looking forward to it.'

Daniel's second date set a precedent for many more Saturdays to come, and he managed to laugh at how he had 'smashed his third date record'. He loved spending time with Zoe, and it was clearly reciprocated, as he met her family and her friends, and they began to spend more and more nights together. We never talked about his sex life – it would have been too excruciating for him – but I hoped that his increasing ease with his body meant that sex would become more intimate for him too.

Daniel trusted that Zoe wasn't going to reject him, and he lost the habit of protecting himself against this risk by convincing the world that he was both clever and 'fine'. I no longer steeled myself for the hard work of our sessions together, and really looked forward to hearing about how his relationship with Zoe was unfolding. I helped him think through his concerns about her and enjoyed hearing his thoughts about her feelings.

One week, he spoke at length of how he was supporting Zoe with her preoccupations about a thirteen-year-old boy who had begun to refuse to go to school. An immigrant from Benin, he was overweight and had a hearing aid, and had been frequently picked on by kids in his class. Daniel's warmth and consideration for the young boy seemed to create a valuable backdraught in the direction of his bullied and lonely younger self.

'I couldn't bear to hear about what he'd been through. He told Zoe about the "meanies" making fun of his weight, his accent, his deafness. I know what that feels like and I don't want him to feel the same.'

Soon after this conversation, Daniel told me that he wanted to finish therapy the following week. I never like finishing therapy so abruptly with clients, but it had the benefit, for Daniel, of circumventing an opportunity to tell me how he had experienced our conversations, and my part in them. Although he avoided any potential intimacy within our relationship, I had high hopes that he'd found this deeper connection with Zoe. She would help him to understand how likeable, and lovable, he actually was. The bullies wouldn't succeed after all.

Chapter Three

Untethered

... striving to look carefree and happy can interfere with your ability to feel so.

JIA TOLENTINO,
Trick Mirror

In the early noughties, when I was in the late stage of my training as a psychotherapist, I worked for a charity that offered counselling in a deprived part of London. I saw a young woman who was repeatedly hurt by her boyfriend's bewildering behaviour and wanted to gain the strength to leave him. For weeks we unpicked their fraught conversations, his unpredictable moods and her conflicted feelings towards him. But I had no idea until shortly before we ended our work that, despite the intensity of their exchanges, the couple had never touched each other: they had met gaming online, and then fallen in love over Skype.

The creases around my eyes make it clear that I'm a digital immigrant: for most of my life, my interactions with other human beings were unmediated by a virtual world. These sessions with a love-struck young adult were a short and sharp lesson about the strength of online relationships. Before then, I tended to minimise them as lesser than the ones I knew best: those between people in the same physical space. But I learned that a meaningful bond *could* be forged through two screens, and I was encouraged to try it myself. I have successfully worked online with clients who have moved abroad, become housebound or have otherwise been unable to make it to my consulting room.

This prepared me well for the pandemic, when social interacting in many forms – including talking therapies – moved online. But well before this catastrophe reconfigured our lives, I was contacted by Marnie, who wanted to meet over FaceTime. She was so time-poor she couldn't afford the hour-long return journey to my room as well as our session time. During a lengthy email exchange before our first virtual meeting, she told me she was 'feeling a mess' because she had run out of ideas about what could help her feel happier. A relationship had recently ended, she loathed her job and 'couldn't stop feeling miserable', however hard she tried.

'I've tried yoga and acupuncture, which calms me for a bit, but never for long, and I'm terrible at meditation. My mind won't ever shut up: there are too many thoughts buzzing around. A friend recommended a clean-eating diet some nutritionist on Insta sells, which is supposed to be good for mental health, but it's so difficult to keep up. I think I need to talk to someone other than my family or friends. If you had any space to see me, that would be amazing! Thank you, Marnie xxx'

There was a time when an 'xxx' sign-off at the end of an enquiry would have felt too familiar, and frankly inappropriate, for the serious work of therapy. But I have had to catch up with how digital natives communicate online, including the importance and meanings of likes, followers, visits, mentions and sign-off kisses. Therapists used to despair about all of this, believing that a client was *avoiding* a relationship when they made contact through the digital, rather than spoken, word. But I wasn't fazed by Marnie's overly familiar sign-off, and guessed she had been in a hurry.

The first time we met, on FaceTime via my laptop and Marnie's phone, there was plenty for me to notice: her neon pink hair was draped around one side of her neck; her nose and upper lip were both pierced with a small silver hoop; and her delicate face was artfully made up. A perfectly symmetrical little tick emerged from the outer corner of each eye. After saying hello, she immediately left her phone to grab something, leaving me to take in piles of clothes, a small jungle of house plants, moving boxes stacked on top of each other and the edge of a hat stand. She had asked to see me before work, on the one day she didn't have to be in the office at her usual early start time.

Working online makes the carefully curated interior of my consulting room redundant. Clients bring their own spaces to me via their devices – kitchens, sitting rooms, bedrooms, studios, the insides of cars and quiet spots in public parks. Before saying much, Marnie gave me a lot to think about, including an immediate sense of disarray. Once she was still again, she began to talk softly, but fast.

'I'm not sure how to do this as I haven't spoken to a therapist before, but a friend suggested it. And I don't know what to talk about first, as I know we only have fifty minutes. But there's so much going on right now and I don't know what's useful or not for you to know.'

Marnie seemed far more fragile than her bold image conveyed, and as soon as she spoke her eyes filled with tears. I worked hard to keep up.

'What feels to be the nearest or the biggest thing to start with?'

'Sorry, I just need to find some tissues. It's so stupid of me not to think of that before. I'm such a douchebag. I know I bought some this week, so they are here somewhere.'

This time, she took her phone with her. While continuing to speak, she darted around her room, with me in virtual tow, picking things up and putting other things down in her quest for tissues. I had to shut my eyes so as not to feel dizzy, opening them when I heard her voice again.

'Nothing feels right. I used to be on top of things, but I can't seem to do anything well any more. Basically, I found out that my ex cheated on me at the same time we moved into a flat together. I borrowed his iPad, and he hadn't un-synced his messages and it was plain to see what had been going on. I can't help wanting to be with him, even though I know he's not worth it. But I moved out and I'm back living with my mum again.'

Marnie turned around, taking me with her again, spreading out her free arm. She gestured towards the chaos, while carrying on at full throttle.

'Welcome to my old bedroom! I still have exam certificates and photos of me and my school mates on the walls. I love this room and my family to bits, but it's small and it's hectic here. They have their own stuff going on right now and it's not ideal timing, my staying. The last thing they need is my gloom around the house. I've been here for four months, and it's beginning to do my head in.'

Marnie propped her phone up so that it was still, and I relaxed a little. She expertly patted her tears away with her tissue without smudging her eyeliner – she would later tell me that she usually detested looking at herself for too long, but her digital reflection gave her one tiny advantage: she could keep her make-up intact.

I needed a moment to take in everything I'd seen and heard, but Marnie pressed on, uneasy with my silence.

'Alex is in my head all the time, and I can't move on. He's still with this other girl, and I sort of know her through work, which makes it all so much worse as she pops up everywhere like bloody Tinkerbell. She's a model and' – Marnie made air quotes – '"an influencer" too. So that makes me feel really good about myself. Not.'

'I'm really sorry, Marnie. How could you not feel hurt – what a betrayal. It sounds like you are still making sense of why he did it. I bet you're having many conversations with him in your head.'

'Yes! Whenever I have a gap from thinking about work. However many times I tell myself, or other people tell me, that I'm better off without him, the fact remains that he chose to be with someone else instead of me. I'm not enough for him. There must be something wrong with me.'

I never like hearing self-evaluations like this. But there is worth in letting words hang sometimes, without challenge, rather than trying to cheer someone up with a platitude. I wanted Marnie to know that I understood how crappy she felt. Feelings of worthlessness inspired by a relationship break-up often permeate other aspects of our lives – it's hard to feel good about ourselves if we have been rejected by a lover.

'What else? You said there was a lot going on for you right now.'

Marnie stood up again, taking her phone across the room so she could retrieve its charger, and then she sat on her bed. Apologising again for not being organised enough (and muttering 'Marnie get it together'), she plugged her phone in and then arranged a number of pillows behind her to support her back. I had to shut my eyes again.

'Marnie, I wonder if it's possible for you to prop up your phone, so that my view of you is stationary? I find it difficult to take in what you are saying when I'm moved around, and it's important I hear it all.'

'Sorry, Julia. I wasn't comfortable there; I should have set myself up properly before. Just to let you know, though, I've got a work meeting that I have to be at, so would you mind if we ended a little early? I'll make sure it won't happen next time. I'm just going to have to pause you to order a cab. One moment.'

I didn't have a chance to protest before Marnie disappeared and I was left staring at a fuzzy screen. Then she was back again.

'Done! Sorry.'

'What's the meeting? Can you tell me a little about your job?'

'It's an editorial catch-up we have each week. I write about events for an online magazine – gigs, shows, exhibitions, launches of new brands and things like that. I've just started doing interviews as well. I started as an intern, and then got an assistant job for a couple of years. This was supposed to be my dream job. At long last I have a proper salary and I get to write. But I don't think I can do it. Even before Alex and I split up, I was starting to get really stressed about it.'

'What are your worries?'

'That I shouldn't have got the job at all. That I'm winging it and any minute someone is going to find out, or maybe they already know that I'm crap and they just haven't come clean with me yet. Honestly, I have nearly resigned so many times – I've got an email sitting in my draft folder that I keep editing. I'd rather hand in my resignation than get found out and sacked … But then I have no idea what else I would do. I've thought about voluntary work abroad or retraining as a teacher but I'm not sure I really want to do either of those things … Sorry Julia, we're going to have to finish! My cab's here.'

I can also fall into a trap of believing I'm not doing a good job. I briefly wondered if I'd failed to capture Marnie's attention and if this was why she couldn't focus more. Perhaps I'd been bland, or even irritated her by insisting she sit still. But while my now occasional habit of self-recrimination exists, I am able to choose whether to be persuaded by it. It seemed that Marnie had a way to go before she could do the same.

I regularly meet people, like Marnie, tussling with so-called imposter syndrome. It's a common means by which self-criticism plays out and is very effective at undermining our confidence, usually in a professional context. I've seen it in perfectionists who question their overall competence after getting one thing (even slightly) wrong, and in those who have sailed through years of high achieving with little trouble and are then hit hard by a storm that challenges them. I've also met supremely self-reliant imposters who feel fraudulent for

having to ask for help, and others who push themselves hard
to succeed in all aspects of their lives in order to prove they
aren't fakes.

I couldn't yet know why or how Marnie's sense of her
professional fraudulence had emerged, nor why Alex's
undeniably hurtful behaviour had caused her to believe that
there was something wrong with her. The words she used to
describe herself and the tone of voice they came in hinted at
the depths of her self-reproach.

Just as I was getting used to Marnie's frenetic pace, she surprised me a few weeks in by appearing on screen with no
energy at all. Sitting at her desk, speaking through her laptop
this time, she looked younger than her twenty-six years, and
far more beautiful. She had no make-up on and had removed
her piercings. I welcomed the calmness her flattened mood
brought, as it allowed me to be with her in a more immediate
way, rather than my usual efforts to chase after her and then
catch up. Tears leaked out of her eyes before I had a chance
to say anything.

'Sorry, Julia. I'm not sure I'm going to be of any use today.'

'I don't need you to be of "use", Marnie, but it would help
for me to know what's going on for you right now.'

She wiped her tears with her fingers. She had no mascara
to worry about this time.

'I don't think I can do this any more.'

Holding my breath and really hoping she didn't mean life,
or even our therapy, I asked, 'What's the "this"?'

'My job. I've just finished writing up an interview, but it's
complete crap. I've been up all night doing it and I have to file
it in an hour, but I really don't think it's in any shape to send.'

Desperate to make her feel better, I offered a nugget of useless reassurance.

'You made your deadline – every editor wants that, surely.'

'But that's not the problem! I feel sick at the thought of my editor reading it. What I've written is rubbish.'

'What will happen if you file a rubbish interview?'

'It could be the tipping point, the piece of work that exposes me as a bad journalist. I will be found out at long last and given my marching orders.'

I wanted to know if her fears were entirely in her imagination or had some basis in truth. I also wanted her to think about the difference between the two.

'Has your writing been criticised before? Sometimes criticisms can sting for far too long.'

Marnie shook her head and spoke unusually slowly. 'No. Not really. But I managed to get away with a lot in the past because I was a junior member of staff, and people tend to be more forgiving of them. But I can't get away with it any more. For so long I have felt like I'm going to get a tap on my shoulder. It's exhausting. I hold my breath every time I see an email from my boss.'

I could see a mug and a couple of empty cans of Coke Zero on the desk beside Marnie, and I knew that sleep deprivation was contributing to her feeling so wretched – none of us do our best thinking when our brain isn't rested. So I decided to offer some immediate practical help, rather than dig into her psyche. I wanted her to pause from feeling such a failure and gather some strength.

'Would it help for me to read through your draft with you?'

Though it's perhaps unusual for a therapist to step into other roles, I will do so at times if I think it's the most effective help I can offer. I've helped clients hone their presentation skills and think through CVs and draft letters. I have also given my – solicited – opinion on a number of personal and professional choices. One advantage of having therapy online is the ability to share material that would be less immediately available in the consulting room – such as photos, messages or documents.

When offering my support in arguably non-therapeutic ways, like reading Marnie's interview, I can't offer the neutrality I usually strive for. Therapists work hard to keep their biases out of the way: we prioritise getting to know the minds of our clients and helping them to think in *their* way. I make it clear that I'm offering an opinion of one person who is trying hard to respect my client's views. With Marnie, I thought a virtual hand-holding exercise like this could at least help her see some of the wood for the trees.

'Thank you but no thank you. I can't bear the idea of you or anyone reading it – it needs far more work. I'm so sorry, Julia, I should have said, but I'm going to have to finish early again.'

Before I had a chance to have more time with her, Marnie's mind had already wandered, fretting over her imagined substandard work and the dire consequences of being found out as incompetent and/or a fake. I already had a pretty good sense of the perfectionism that felled her: the standards she set for herself were very high, and she couldn't tolerate not reaching them. I'd lost count of the times she referred to herself as an imbecile or stupid for not remembering something or for making a small mistake.

Marnie's not the first millennial I've met who pushes herself hard. A number of studies have found that this cohort suffer from mental ill health far more than Baby Boomers and Generation X-ers (of which I am one), with high rates of eating disorders, anxiety, depression and suicidal ideation. One influential study by leading psychologists tested the idea that these mental health problems could be partly explained by the excessive standards that young people set for themselves, and the subsequent self-punishment that follows when they don't achieve them.* This study tracked 41,641 American, Canadian and British students who were at college between 1989 and 2016 and it concluded that their levels of perfectionism, broadly defined as 'a combination of excessively high personal standards and overly critical self-evaluations', had increased over the two decades, by statistically significant amounts. The psychologists speculated that this may be because 'generally, American, Canadian, and British cultures have become more individualistic, materialistic, and socially antagonistic over this period, with young people now facing more competitive environments, more unrealistic expectations, and more anxious and controlling parents than generations before'. This research backed up other studies that suggest that perfectionism, self-criticism and poor mental health are interlinked – and many therapists know this to be the case too.

When we next met, Marnie had bounced back to her more usual, effervescent self. She didn't mention her great distress about her interview, which had dominated our previous session, and soon after greeting each other we were both

---

* T. Curran and A. P. Hill, 2019. 'Perfectionism is increasing over time: A meta-analysis of birth cohort differences from 1989 to 2016', *Psychological Bulletin*, 145(4), 410.

distracted by raised voices outside her room. I wanted to pick up on her ability to flip from great upset to a sunny self, which I had seen at other times, but I also didn't want to miss an opportunity to satisfy my curiosity about her family.

Marnie often referred to her parents and siblings when she told me about her week, and she seemed very involved with all of their lives. Her digital devices kept her plugged into a tight family network, but her emotional ties clearly did too. The task of adolescence – which is about separating ourselves from our caregivers to become fully independent – lasts longer than we used to think. We now know that our brains are busy rewiring themselves until at least our mid-twenties, so at twenty-six, Marnie was still teetering at the edges of adulthood, however capable and intelligent she was.

I had already sort of met Marnie's parents. Once we had agreed to meet regularly, she had introduced me, over email, to four people, and gave them the details of my bank account. Her mother and father, and their respective partners, would be taking it in turn to pay my fees – an early signal to me of their equitable and friendly co-parenting relationship since divorcing when Marnie was a toddler. But it also confirmed to me that Marnie had not fully flown the nest.

'Is everything okay right now? We can both hear an impressive argument going on.'

Marnie sent her eyes heavenward and smiled. It was something she was used to.

'That's Mum and my sister. They aren't getting on at the moment. But the house should be empty any minute now. I'll sort them out later!'

Asking about her household let me find out more about

her family tree – sometimes I ask a client to draw one, which can reveal lots about relationships between members. After Marnie and Alex had split up, she had returned to live with her mother, her stepfather and her teenage half-sisters. She was speaking to me from the home where she had spent half of her time growing up, with the rest of her time spent at her father's house. He had married his second wife when Marnie was twelve, and they had two sons. Marnie was the eldest child of both her mother and father, and their only one together.

'Mum and Dad were best friends before they had me, and they are still best friends. They just could never be lovers.'

Marnie described them endearingly, but also in a slightly exasperated way, just as she had her four younger siblings. She seemed to be saying that she was the steady member of a slightly chaotic group.

'They lived on the same road for years after they divorced, but Dad moved further away after he had the boys. Although I'd share my time equally between them, it got a bit muddled after the girls came along, as they would often come with me to stay at Dad's, and then the boys would come with me to Mum's sometimes. My parents all work super hard, so they helped each other out a lot. I know it sounds odd to be such a blended family – no one understands it really! It would be far easier if we all lived together in one big house.'

It makes sense that, as a therapist, I'd hear far more stories of unhappy family separations than happy ones, and while Marnie's experience didn't strike me as odd, the dynamic she described wasn't that familiar to me. She spoke of Christmases, birthdays and camping trips with both family sets bundled together as if they were one, and sometimes she referred to her stepfather Mike as 'Dad' and her stepmother Chloe as 'Mum'. Less unusually, her siblings were never distanced by the addition of the word half.

I didn't want to dull the powerful glow that Marnie created as she spoke of her 'mega-family', but as she described her parents meeting their new partners and having more children, I imagined a young Marnie, always on the move between her two homes. As she stepped across the threshold she would have adjusted herself to each family system and environment. It made sense that she wanted everyone to live together and nestle into one coherent home.

'Not everyone I know enjoys being the eldest of a sibling group. What was it like for you?'

'Sometimes I feel like an extra parent! All the sibs turn to me when they need advice or help with negotiations with the parents, and especially the girls. I had to fight the battles first of course – curfews, piercings, festivals, boyfriends. But I feel very close to them as I have looked after them quite a bit over the years. I'd earn my allowance babysitting, cooking meals, helping with their homework, walking them to school.'

'It sounds like you have been very involved.'

'I could always see how hard my parents worked to provide for us, and they supported me through so many of my whims and interests. Being helpful is the least I could do and can do.'

I wondered if Marnie's high standards had been set at an early age. Being helpful is a commendable trait in any child but stepping up to take responsibility for other family members is best left to the adults.

'You told me that you would sort out the argument we heard outside your room. Do you do much of that?'

'Oh yes! I'm always the one to sort out squabbles. But to be fair, I'm also a bit of a control freak, so I do take it upon myself to be the mediator.'

Marnie went on to tell me about a childhood of 'control freakery' – or in my mind, a desire to 'do' all the time – that made me weary even to hear about. From the age of seven she swam in a local competitive squad, with training before school, while in the afternoons she took acting, dance and saxophone classes. At secondary school she took up athletics, played in the orchestra and co-edited the school newspaper. She was popular and thrived academically, ending up with the grades to study philosophy at a prestigious university.

As she spoke of the pace of her life growing up, I couldn't compute how she fitted everything in, alongside her busy role in the mega-family. Growing up in the seventies and eighties, I had little to do in my free time but play, often in nearby streets with other kids who roamed around, a bit filthy, like me. Children's TV and extracurricular activities were thin on the ground, and our parents left us to get on with it, ignoring our pleas of boredom or the fact they knew little of what we were up to.

Marnie clearly knew how to *do* but struggled to know how to just *be*. I wanted to check out how much her quest to achieve came from genuine passions and desires, as opposed to, as I suspected, a fear of not being good enough. She was primed to judge herself harshly if she wasn't pursuing and achieving goals: while she carved out a role as a capable, dependable, high-achieving self who no one need worry about, she was keeping a self-critic at bay.

'It sounds like you have always had a lot of plates to spin. Did any of them ever drop and smash?'

Marnie smiled and sighed at the same time.

'I don't drop plates! There's a breakfast cereal called Golden Morn that my mum used to eat as a child. She called me Golden Marn because I was her golden girl – always reliable and never any bother. She says she never had to worry about me. I'm still called Goldie by lots of people now.'

'I wonder if you would have dropped a plate if you hadn't been anointed Golden Marn?'

Marnie took time to consider the removal of her gilding.

'I don't think so. I was encouraged to do loads of activities and my parents were always busy too. I grew up being told that I should just try to do my best. So I did just that – I tried to do my best – at a lot of things! Hang on a minute, I've just thought of something.'

Marnie walked away and rustled through bags, alongside repeatedly apologising for her visual absence. She returned holding a small rectangular piece of frayed linen, embroidered with colourful child-like stitching, and held it up to the camera.

'I made this in year five, and I pinned it on the wall in this room. But then I took it to hang up in the flat that Alex and I moved into. I was going to frame it.'

. Nine-year-old Marnie had stitched the words 'I will always do my best' with 'best' beaming out in bright pink capital letters. Knowing that she didn't do anything by halves, I imagined her intense focus as she carefully stitched this talisman. But while aspiring to follow the mantra kept her role as Golden Marn intact, its objective of BEST couldn't ever be objectively fixed, and it kept Marnie striving.

'Do you know what your best means?' I asked. 'We each have a different best to judge ourselves by and mine will be different from yours. For example, I've learned that my best may even be a so-called fail at times.'

'I have no idea any more. All I know is that I'm far away from doing my best. In fact, I feel I'm doing my worst.'

Marnie's feeling that she was 'doing her worst' was confirmed to me by her drooping shoulders and extra-quiet tone. While Marnie's words were important, I always worked to attune to the way she spoke them, along with noting changes in her skin tone, eye movements and breathing. Even the subtlest of clues from someone's body language or appearance can suggest how they are feeling.

I wished Marnie was in the room with me in this moment of vulnerability. As much as I believe that meaningful bonds can be forged online, I don't think that they can replace the feeling of meeting someone in person, in the consulting room or elsewhere. We all have the ability, via our breathing and eye contact, to help regulate each other's nervous systems and emotional worlds. There's a powerful, unseen feedback loop of arousal and soothing that happens between humans that is far easier in the flesh. In my online sessions with Marnie, I could only do my best.

Marnie hung on in there at work, enduring her frequent fear of being 'busted'. I wasn't surprised to hear that the interview she had been so anxious about had gone down well with her editor, and that its publication had thousands of hits and shares. She'd gained scores of new followers on her social media channels, including the celebrity interviewee himself, who had messaged her to thank her for her measured and intelligent prose.

Despite all the praise and plentiful digital thumbs-ups, Marnie was buoyed only briefly, and she quickly returned to criticising herself for another substandard piece of work, and for delivering it so close to the wire. Any type of praise, flattery or complimentary feedback needs a measure of self-love to latch on to, and then to saturate through.

Marnie frequently referred to the parallel virtual existence that her colleagues, friends and family occupied. Her anecdotes moved interchangeably between online interactions and events and those in real life, and when she spoke to me from her laptop her phone was always to hand. If she spoke to me from her phone, there'd usually be another device near by. But these digital pacifiers could also be her tormentors.

'I know I shouldn't do it, but after reading comments about my interview I found myself scrolling through profiles of other journalists and people that I don't even know, and then I'm sucked into their lives. I can't help myself – even though I *know* that when I do this I always end up feeling ugly or boring or not successful enough. And I always end up checking what Alex is up to, and his new bloody beautiful girlfriend.'

Lives as depicted on social media are often distorted and unrealisable. None of us actually lead carefully curated – and colour-filtered – 'Insta-friendly' lives. I have had many conversations in my consulting room about the 'comparing and despairing' phenomenon that affects so many of my clients – of all ages, even though it bites young people the most.

Marnie had created a big social media presence for herself, and her job meant she had to keep tabs on competitor journalists, celebrities and trends emerging among her fellow millennials and the younger Gen Z. All of her friends and family managed a full-time online existence too. I had quickly stopped trying to discern whether conversations she referred to had been said in person or through messages typed with thumbs – it didn't matter much, bar Marnie's propensity to read more into, and worry more about, images she saw and words that she read, rather than those which had been spoken.

I strive to keep my relationships with my clients within the confines of my consulting room, or as was the case with Marnie, within our shared digital space. I never looked at her social media presence. The therapeutic frame is crucial to the potential success of the work, as it emphasises my professional role. Everything that makes up the parameters of our relationship helps to maintain it too: the fifty-minute session, the set time each week, the payment of my fee, my consistent consulting room or digital background, as well as my decision to keep the details of my life private. This also means that I choose not to be a client's friend, even when we finish our therapy sessions.

I had learned quite a bit about how Marnie depicted herself offline, but I was intrigued to understand more about how she did this in her digital realm and because of my boundaries I couldn't find out without her showing me.

'I've heard about how Instagram gets you down, but I'd love to see how you participate in it too. Do you mind showing me?'

I suspected she tried hard to be golden online too. After a moment of tapping, she lifted her phone up to the laptop camera so I could see her profile and feed. These daily posts betrayed nothing of the total lack of belief in herself that I knew she often felt. If anything, her stream of selfies – requisite pout included – conveyed a young woman who was assured and at ease.

Every image of her beautiful face cried out, 'Yay! This is all so great!', and with a critical mass of followers, she was now prey to being monetised: brands had sent her items to wear and show off to her chorus. As she explained all of this to me, she grabbed a handful of lipsticks that had been sent her way.

'Marnie, what's it like, showing me this online version of you? It seems so very different from the you that I'm getting to know, who seems so wary of believing in herself. I see no sign of a self-critic in those images of you.'

'Hah! I think I look *so* rough. There's not one single photo here that I like. I know it's all a performance, but I need to do it for work. Building a social media profile means more people read my writing, and that's good for the magazine and for my status there.'

I've never met anyone who criticises themselves ferociously but also feels good about their physical appearance – although they may feel much better about their *adjusted* bodies after putting in a great effort: nips and tucks, diet and exercise, hair dye, on-trend clothes and make-up. Marnie's own efforts seemed to make no difference to her confidence, and I knew that her addiction to social media was chipping away at the little amount of self-esteem that she had.

Marnie then bit her lip and added,

'I guess I also want Alex to see I'm fine without him.'

Sometimes an obvious suggestion can be the most therapeutic.

'How would it be to have some time off social media? Or even your phone? Could you turn it off for a day or two as an experiment to see how it affects how you feel?'

Her cat-like eyes widened and she smiled.

'I don't even know how to turn my phone off.'

I thought she was joking, but she wasn't.

*

Alex was never far from Marnie's mind when we spoke each week. Her broken heart was not mending as fast as she had hoped, and she wasn't ready to date again, despite the encouragement of her friends and family. She downloaded dating apps but couldn't face the self-marketing that they demanded. Selling her brand online was far easier for her than selling her dating self and her self-critic reared up every time she even thought of assembling a profile.

We had discussed over and again how her addiction to scrolling served to undermine her already shaky self-worth. She knew social media posts became instruments of self-torture, partly because they also drip-fed her details of Alex's new life and love. Frustrated as I was at her apparent reluctance to help herself by taking a break from her phone, she was at last slowing down a bit in our sessions, allowing herself more time to think and note her feelings. At least with me she became more able to just be rather than do, shown by her toleration of the occasional silence between us.

Many clients dislike a lull in conversation because it risks exposing an uncomfortable critical inner narrative; some have told me that a silence tells them that they are boring me, or not doing therapy right. I had been leaving silences as opportunities for Marnie to hear her inner recriminations, and when she did speak, I would point out how they would often leak out onto me: 'You are going to think I'm ridiculous . . . ' or 'This is going to sound crazy . . . ' or 'I bet you are bored of hearing this . . . '

Even though Marnie was easing into a slower pace, I was surprised when she began one of our meetings with a long silence. There had been the one time we had met with her in tears, but she had never been so quiet. I was used to bracing

myself for a torrent of words as she caught me up with her diz-
zyingly busy and heavily populated life. After a few minutes
of looking away from the camera, fiddling with something
out of my view, she sheepishly confessed.

'I feel terrible about this, and you are going to want to give
up on me now. I just did a series of stupid things and I've got
no one to blame but myself.'

Said like a true self-critic.

'Let me hear what happened.'

Marnie had spent another weekend on the move with
friends, going from one bar to another to another. Feeling
my age, I marvelled at her capacity to socialise so much after
her punishingly long working week, and then to function on
barely any sleep, nor any time on her own. Her Friday night
had begun early, and she drank cocktails, got drunk and
then high.

'I'm so embarrassed to tell you all of this. But I completely
lost the plot, and I hooked up with some bloke that I vaguely
know. At the time, I thought it would do some good, that it
would help get Alex out of my head. My best friend likes to
remind me that Mae West said that the best way to get over
somebody is to get under somebody else.'

Clearly uncomfortable, Marnie was sketchy with the
details of what had happened between them, but it didn't
sound much fun.

'I came home feeling dreadful, and then it hit me how I
hadn't wanted to be there, and how I just wanted to be with
Alex in our old life together. I couldn't help myself: even with
your voice in my head telling me not to, I started scrolling.
Sure enough, I saw pictures of loads of people I know in our
flat – *his* flat now. And then I saw pictures of his girlfriend in

the bedroom that was briefly ours. It looks like she's moved in: her stuff was everywhere.'

'Ah, that sucks, Marnie. I'm sorry you saw all that.'

'I'm a moth to a flame when it comes to shitty partners. But I have now actually done it! At very long last I've deleted him from everywhere possible. I hope you are pleased with me.'

I was pleased, of course, but I wanted to return to her comment about 'shitty partners'. I don't always feel protective of my clients, nor do I automatically take their side in relationship spats or break-ups. I was taught early on to harbour scepticism alongside a belief in a client's version of truth, to bear in mind that there is always more than one version of a story, and that every relationship is a co-creation. But I found Marnie so likeable that I couldn't shake off my inclination to believe that she *had* been treated badly.

'Tell me about your shitty partners.'

'I may be Golden Marn in a lot of ways, but never in the love department. I was with a boy from fifteen until eighteen, who, looking back, treated me really badly. He would dump me every few months, break my heart, and then I'd always take him back. He had problems at home with his mum, who was an alcoholic, so I always felt sorry for him and ended up forgiving him. I really helped him with his GCSEs too as he was always behind.'

'Now I hear of another person you were looking after in your teens.'

'I don't think it stopped there either because at uni I had my first relationship with a woman. She was a hedonist and great fun at first, and she helped me regain my confidence in many ways – she was the one who dyed my hair this colour! But then she developed an eating disorder, so it became quite intense between us. I was doing everything I could to help her out, taking her to the doctor, getting psychological support, making eating plans with her. She left uni one day without any warning, and completely ghosted me – she still owes me lots of money. I was single for ages after that, apart from the odd crappy one-night stand. And then I met Alex three years ago.'

She looked directly into the camera, as if into my eyes.

'And here I am now.'

It seemed that Marnie was beginning to see a pattern of relationships that had worked against her. In looking at me in the way she did, it seemed that she knew that I knew she had long believed she deserved only crumbs rather than the cake.

Sometimes a client tells me of a seemingly trivial incident that turns out to have a disproportionate effect upon them. For Marnie, this was forgetting to take her phone on a weekend away.

Her father's birthday was coming up, and the mega-family planned to gather in a hotel by the sea in Cornwall to celebrate. We had talked about this event in some detail, as it reflected the many happy summer holidays Marnie had spent at the same place as a child. She realised that she hadn't been able to relax during those summer gatherings, either because she was looking after a sibling or because she was pursuing some extracurricular assignment.

'I'd always be teased for packing the most – I'd lug along an art project to work on or an instrument to practise or a pile of books to read. I was never carefree.'

Ironically, on this recent visit Marnie didn't take enough. In a tearing hurry to leave the house in time, she left her phone behind.

'I can't remember *ever* doing that before. My phone is glued to me, as you well know. But by the time I realised, we were already on the motorway and Mum wasn't going to turn back – it's an epic journey. I was in a complete panic, but when we eventually got to the sea I felt a bit better. I realised I could borrow other people's phones to check crucial things.

In the morning, as I was having a shower, I noticed that I felt unusually calm and it took a while to work out why. On waking, I hadn't immediately grabbed my phone and started scrolling. I usually begin my day looking at what I've missed out on or worrying about something I posted before I went to sleep.'

'That sounds liberating!'

'It was just so obvious how neither my head nor my heart was racing. I had a brilliant weekend in the end – it ended up being the digital detox you suggested. I slept loads, I ate well, and you know what? I sat back a bit and practised just letting my family get on with it. When Mum and my sister began to tussle I got up and walked away. I actually said, "I'm going to leave you guys to this."'

'So you didn't try to do your best as a mediator.'

'Exactly! It was difficult though. I really wanted to. And then I went for a swim, and I just swam until I didn't want to any more. I didn't set myself a goal to swim to a certain rock or to practise my crawl or to time myself.'

Forgetting her phone may not have been the sole cause of Marnie's unprecedented inner ease, but it seemed to have helped quieten her inner critic and reduce the pressure it exerted on her to do and do well.

'By leaving your mum and sister to it, you practised something new – attending to yourself instead – and it sounds like it went okay. I'm guessing your mum and sister survived their squabble? And you'll still be Goldie, even though you didn't save them or swim to the rocks in an impressive time?'

Marnie smiled, understanding what I was driving at.

'This bodes well for the next time you have a chance to ease up on yourself. But it also means slowing down enough to recognise when you have that chance.'

It took some weeks of practising, with my help from the wings, but Marnie did learn to increasingly allow for quiet moments, during which she could recognise and investigate her urge to push herself and take on too much. She could see how her frantic pace of life, baked in early on by her efforts to please her two-in-one family, had ultimately worked against her ability to build a self-worth that began on the inside.

After we spoke for the final time, I was more confident that Marnie's best had become a more settled notion, rather than the unattainable – and moveable – goal it had previously been. She was increasingly able to cut herself some slack, which meant doing more and more without an impulse to achieve.

Chapter Four

Man Up

This above all: to thine own self be true,
And it must follow, as the night the day,
Thou canst not then be false to any man.

Polonius,
in SHAKESPEARE,
Hamlet

Jason didn't show up for our first meeting. I left a message on his phone and thought of other clients who had missed initial meetings and remained ambivalent about the therapy that followed. Of course, 'Do Not Attends' also happen without meaning anything, as a result of a genuine error. I've misrecorded dates in my diary many times when hurried, distracted or anxious, and I don't believe these were all unconscious attempts to avoid what I was attempting to commit to. Even Freud was said to have noted that sometimes a cigar is just a cigar.

Jason rescheduled for the following week by email, rather

than phoning me back. It was hard to detect any hesitation about coming to meet me when at last I opened the door to him. He was holding his head with both hands, in a pose of remorse. He still seemed horrified at letting me down, even though I had already received a fulsome apology, and a prompt settling of my fee as my cancellation policy requests. He said he was delighted to finally meet with me and made a point of looking me straight in the eye while he held my hand in a firm handshake.

'It's great to meet you, Julia: thank you for finding the time for me again. I can't apologise enough for my no-show.'

He looked tired, and the force of his charm seemed effortful. I meet many men who stride purposefully into my room ahead of me, but Jason wasn't one of them. He let me lead the way and then didn't know whether to sit on my sofa or one of the two chairs. Although my boundaries with my clients are pretty set, I don't have a particular seat in my consulting room. I prefer to follow my client's lead and then seat myself not too close or too far away. Often, a choice of seat reveals something to think about: spreading out on the large sofa is different from perching on the edge of a chair.

I relieved Jason of his indecision by suggesting a chair with higher sides, thinking he'd find it containing. His email had said nothing of what was on his mind, so I invited him to let me know.

'My girlfriend Kate and I have been having problems for a while now, and she suggested that we each have our own personal therapy to see if that would help us sort things out. I'm afraid I have no idea how all of this works, though, but I owe it to her to give this a try. Please feel free to ask me anything.'

Jason raised his hands in a gesture of openness that didn't

quite convince me. He acted as if he was willingly in the room but betrayed a discomfort too – he hadn't taken his long blue wool coat off, though it wasn't cold. I often meet people describing themselves as open and who are indeed good at telling stories of their experiences, but at the same time they resist thinking about how these experiences may have impacted them.

'Tell me more about your problems with Kate. Just to remind you of the obvious, she's not here now, and I won't ever meet her, so please talk as freely as you can.'

Some therapists are happy to bring in the other half of a couple after a few weeks of meeting with a client. I can't trust that I would be completely impartial, so I make it a policy not to do this. Clients have turned up with their partner without any warning, and I have had to spell out my inevitable bias in favour of my client. These sessions rank highly in my list of the most awkward ones I've experienced.

Jason began, 'Kate is one of the loveliest people I know. I love her to bits, but I don't think I can give her what she wants right now. She's been living here temporarily on a work visa and has always planned to return home to Australia. She now has a really good job there and is leaving in three months. We had planned for me to move back home with her, but it's come at the wrong time. I've suggested that I join her later, when I'm clear of this big project I've just taken on at work. She thinks I should leave with her because otherwise I'll never go.'

'And what do you think?'

'I don't know any more. My thinking depends on the time of day. One moment I'm ready to hand in my notice and book my ticket to Australia, but then an hour later I don't want to. I worry about our relationship, and my career.

Sometimes it feels the fairest thing to do is to let her go, especially as she is keen to have a baby. That's another thing I'm not sure about.'

'You are stuck.'

'I am. I love Kate and I hate the idea of letting her down so badly, and of breaking her heart. But I also love what I do and I'm within reach of getting somewhere, at long last. I've had to work so incredibly hard to get this far. We aren't perfect together anyway. I think we – or rather, I – have been ignoring stuff between us for a long time.'

'What sort of stuff?'

'I've been rubbish for the past year or even two, and I can admit that. I've been distracted by work and my photography and other things. I know I've taken her for granted. There's no doubt that she deserves better, including a clear commitment from me.'

Jason leant forwards and rested his forehead in his hands so that he looked down at the floor. I could no longer see his face, only the top of his neatly cut head of hair. His shoulders curled upwards towards his ears and I was taken aback by the sudden change in his demeanour: one moment he was looking at me intensely, the next he had curled inwards like a little boy.

'Something got you there, Jason. Can you tell me what it was?'

When he looked up, I could feel the pain of his tremendous bind but also that he was holding back. He didn't speak of shame, but it looked like he felt it. I didn't want to push him this early on in our relationship, so I went through the other usual questions of an initial session: inquiring into major life events, the history of his mental and physical health, and the details of his family make-up. I knew that his answers might only give me a fraction of what needed to be explored.

When we finished, Jason was in a very different mood from the seemingly upbeat one he had arrived in, and I was unsure as to whether he had any faith that our conversations could help him. Our first encounter seemed only to have heightened the distress of his predicament. As I began to close the door behind him, he looked at me and then shook his head, turned away and ran up the steps to the pavement. There was clearly something bothering Jason that he couldn't yet say. It could have been something about me that put him off, of course, and I suspected he was dealing with a critical voice that told him to hide whatever it was. We had agreed to meet again, but I wouldn't have been surprised had he not returned.

Jason did show up as planned, with the initial enthusiasm he'd conveyed before. I noted how he appeared to have had a parting thought as we said our goodbyes the previous week, but he dismissed it as nothing and was keen to move on to tell me about his project at work, and to answer my questions about his relationship with Kate. She turned out to be his first serious girlfriend. He spoke of a number of fleeting relationships with women in his early twenties, but none that had mattered, and none that he wanted to dwell upon. Aged thirty-two, he had met Kate at the party of a mutual friend soon after she had arrived in London and they had immediately hit it off.

'Everyone loves Kate. She's gorgeous – down-to-earth, fun, clever and super-kind. She's a physiotherapist, so she's all about caring for other people. We were the best of friends for a couple of years and we did everything together. It was her idea for us to become a couple, and I was reluctant at first, which is partly why I feel so dreadful now. I couldn't make my mind up for months and when I eventually agreed to give things a go, I promised her I was a hundred per cent sure. She was in for the long haul from the start. That was a couple of years ago – and that's when I began to be crap. I was a much better friend than lover.'

'Are you still lovers?'

Jason seemed uncomfortable with my question, and confidently reassured me that 'that side of things was okay', as a means to close down further discussion of the topic. Sex is becoming an easier subject of conversation in my consulting room, but it still inspires discomfort. Years ago, I met a French therapist at a conference about couples' therapy. She had recently moved to London and was building her practice but lamented the English reluctance to talk about sex: it made her work painfully slower than the pace she was used to.

'What's going on between us is to do with me, it's nothing to do with her,' Jason continued. 'I guess I've just been too focused on work of late.'

Leaving their sex life until Jason felt more comfortable with me, I asked more about the hard graft of his job, and how he pitched his commitment to Kate against it.

'Why do you think you work so hard?'

'I haven't thought about it, really. I started work when I was sixteen, working with my dad as his apprentice plumber. And then I moved to London when I was eighteen and had to work really hard to keep my head above water – at one point I was working in a call centre in the day and as a security guard at night. I slept on my friend's cousin's sofa. But eventually I made it as a runner in a TV production company.'

Jason had arrived in London wide-eyed and with a determination to work behind the camera. By the time we met,
over fifteen years later, he was well established as a freelance
director in the advertising industry. I was intrigued by his
remarkable journey from plumbing.

'It wasn't just plumbing. I was always focused on becoming
a professional football player. Film was a secret pipe dream,
and football was everything at home. My dad runs the local
club and we pretty much grew up on the pitch. As soon as
we were old enough, we were training every evening, every
weekend and all holidays.'

'We?'

'My brother John and me. John made it as a professional –
you have probably heard of him if you are interested in
football. Sometimes I get mistaken for him, because we look
so alike, even though I'm five years older. He's his club's star
player, and quite outspoken about things. He's getting married to a reality TV star and they get papped when they are
out and about. Which he loves.'

'But you didn't turn professional.'

'I wasn't good enough. John still likes to remind me! It was
clear by the time he was eight or nine that he had the edge. I
wasn't strong enough, or fast enough. But also, the real truth
is that my heart wasn't ever fully in it.'

'That sounds difficult, to be spending all your time pursuing the wrong dream.'

'It was my dad's dream, not mine. He was very proud
of John, and always a little bit annoyed that I didn't have
his talent.'

'Annoyed?'

'He put everything down to practice. He'd often tell me

off for not trying hard enough. Looking back, maybe he was right, because as I said, my heart wasn't completely in it. I always had other interests and he couldn't understand that, especially as John lived, breathed and ate football.'

Hearing Jason say this made me think of the English paediatrician and psychoanalyst Donald Winnicott, whose work I mentioned in the context of 'good-enough mothering' in Charlotte's story. He wrote a number of papers in the sixties that were influential beyond psychotherapists' conversations, including his observations about the healthy and unhealthy development of the 'true self' and 'false self' in infants and children. The former refers to our authentic, unfiltered way of being in the world, which may include our rageful and selfish demands. If a child screams blue murder when her biscuit breaks in two, it helps for her to know that her rage is okay (although she needs to learn how to manage it skilfully), and also that it doesn't destroy her parent.

If all goes well, Winnicott's thinking goes, we also develop a false self as an appropriate check on our potential self-absorption and wildness. We learn to think about and adapt to others' needs. We may still feel rage if our biscuit breaks, but we deal with that feeling privately, and we don't insult or kick the biscuit-giver. However, such a false self is only healthy if it layers upon, and knows of, our true self. Adapting to others is appropriate, but not if it bends us out of shape.

Whenever I hear of a parent's dream overriding a child's, I think of this careful coupling of selves and I often help people to think about this process. It sounded like Jason's football-playing self wasn't true, so this was likely to mean he felt badly about wanting other versions of himself – and this is a common seed for self-criticism to grow from. It couldn't have helped that John, in contrast to Jason, followed their dad's dream alongside him.

'What were your other interests?'

'I always loved cameras and film. My grandma moved in with us after my grandpa died, when I was about six. She loved the cinema and we'd watch films together whenever we could. I also loved being on my own taking photos, I still do. But I had to do everything with or for the team.'

'So when did you give up playing football?'

'I tried out for every club that I could, but I wasn't selected. I was always a nearly but never quite strong enough. I'd often be asked to try again the following year. Then I injured my knee really badly and couldn't play for months. It was all over before I was eighteen.'

Boys can go off the rails if they aren't selected by football clubs after years and years of training – it can be such a disorientating loss of a dream, and of their only known purpose in life. There are charities that step in to help get rejected young men back on their feet, but they can't cope with the demand, and many boys are left broken by a shattered imagined future, and a dire loss of confidence. At least Jason had had other interests to mitigate his loss, and I suspected his grief was bearable.

'How was that ending for you?'

'Well, apart from the knee pain, it was a relief. It was a much bigger loss for Dad though – he was devastated. He had wanted to play professional football as well but had the same knee injury as mine, and when he was seventeen too. Strange, eh? I benefited from better surgery and my knee's okay now – his still bothers him. And then, the following year, John was picked up by a professional club, and Dad's focus switched from immense disappointment in me to pride in him.'

I guessed that his father's constant reminder of his own thwarted ambitions from his own nagging knee, must have fuelled his disappointment.

'How did you know about his immense disappointment?'

Jason chuckled, but it didn't sound natural.

'Dad doesn't mince words. He made it very clear that I had let him down – in his mind, my injury happened because I was in the wrong position in the field. It didn't help that I clearly wasn't going to carry on in the family plumbing business.'

'And what then for you?'

'I'd been apprenticing with Dad after my GCSEs for a year or so, but that wasn't what I wanted. So once my knee was sorted, I took my basic qualifications down to London. Coming here was the final nail in the coffin – he thought I'd betrayed the family, and my working-class roots. He's very proud of where he comes from, as is John.'

'What's it like between you and your father now?'

'Much better than it was. We didn't talk for a very long time, but he's slowly come round. I've tried hard to stay in contact, and to visit when I can. But he's come to London just three times since I moved, and only for the day each time – he hates it here. He left the country for the first time in his life last year, for his sixtieth birthday, and he vowed never to use his passport again. He still can't get his head around what I do, and I'm in a very different world to his.'

Jason dropped his head again, as if he were feeling the force of his father's – and perhaps his brother's – rejection.

'What do you talk about these days, then?'

'Not much. If I call home, he'll say "All right?" before quickly saying, "I'll get your mum," and he's gone. If I can make him talk, it'll be about the club or football or work, but it won't be a two-way conversation. He tends to have a pretty fixed view on things. It works well on the football pitch, or in the pub with his mates, but it makes it impossible to have a dialogue, or a proper relationship with him really. Mum and John seem to manage it, but I never have.'

'He sounds like a "man's man" to me.'

'He is, yes! Men don't show weakness of any kind. When I was about ten, I was tackled badly in a match and, as it turned out, I broke a finger. He took me off the pitch, held me by the shoulders at arm's length, looked me in the eyes and told me to stop crying. I had to go back on and play.'

'Did his instruction work?'

'I suppose so. I do find it hard to cry about anything, and my pain threshold is high. When my knee was injured, the A&E doctor didn't believe it was that serious because I should have been in far more obvious pain. My cruciate ligament had torn, and I barely flinched! Kate would say I'm far too stoic – she wishes I would complain more.'

I guessed that there were many times when Kate wanted Jason to speak up, and to share more of his inner world with her. From our first meeting he had made it clear that there was more to tell me than he had so far. Hearing how he'd been criticised for buckling with the pain of a broken finger made me wonder how he had learned to feel towards other pains – his knee, and also emotional vulnerabilities.

'Did John have to "man up" too?'

'John's a chip off the old block. I'll never know if, underneath it all, he felt pressure from Dad to be tougher than he really is, or whether he is genuinely invincible. He's never been seriously injured. But we don't talk much either: we have always been so different. He's chippy that I left home and makes digs at my London life and my "posh southern accent" whenever I see him. He can't understand why I'd want to live in a tiny flat working such long hours. He runs around outside and lives in a mansion!'

'Has your accent changed, then?'

'I never decided to get rid of it, but it has faded. My industry is full of privileged people, mainly from London or near by and I guess it's rubbed off on me. People often marvel when I tell them I grew up on a northern council estate and left school at sixteen.'

Sometimes we hold on to accents when they mean something positive to us. I had a client who spoke with a strong French accent, despite being born and raised in London. Her French father had died when she was very young. While her three older siblings apparently sounded like true south Londoners, she couldn't let go of this link to the man she had loved so much and still grieved for. But we can shed accents if they feel negative, and I wondered if Jason had unconsciously distanced himself from any marker of his humble roots.

'It's not so good being so "marvellous", as your colleagues would say?'

Jason raised his eyebrows and sighed.

'To be honest, I find it patronising – as if I'm some sort of hero for making it without an Oxbridge degree. I don't have the confidence, or networks, that privilege has given lots of people I know. I can often feel on the edge, not quite fitting in.'

I winced, internally, at hearing this and wondered how Jason felt about my own posh-sounding accent and arguably posh-looking room full of tokens of travel and education. It was important to know if there was any trace of that feeling when he was with me, as a means to explore it further.

'I wonder how you feel about my apparent privilege. Could you imagine that I may think less of you because you aren't in my entitled tribe too?'

Jason seemed surprised by my injection of our relationship into the conversation, as many clients can be. It forces an intimacy that they may not be ready for.

'I may have done in the past. But I'm more forgiving since meeting Kate – she doesn't judge people and, coming from Australia, she has different class filters. She was the first person I introduced to Dad because I knew she would take him with a pinch of salt. He has some pretty provocative views about many things, women and foreigners included.'

I turned my head to the side a little, in anticipation of more.

'We went back to see my parents at Christmas and Dad couldn't understand why she wants to return to Australia for a better job when I've got a good one here. He thinks that men should provide for their wives, just as his own father did, he does, and John probably will. It didn't occur to him that I was thinking of leaving my job.'

'So he's an unlikely sounding board for your dilemma right now.'

'He's an unlikely sounding board for anything. We just don't have that close relationship.'

'I can hear the hurt in your voice as you say that.'

'I know he loves me deeply. And that was why he didn't want to have anything to do with me when I left. I think I broke his heart, and it broke mine too. I've more or less accepted that I'll never be the son he'd hoped me to be and we're okay now.'

The English language uses a number of bodily metaphors to describe emotional pain: criticisms can hurt or bruise us; we can feel gutted by sadness and eviscerated by grief. Language is perhaps wiser than we realise: a number of neuroscience studies show that social rejection – by peers, family members, lovers – triggers the same neural circuits that process physical injury, which, in turn, translates to the experience of pain. One client of mine, perhaps intuiting this, would take a paracetamol on waking to soothe the heartache of her miscarriages.

The social psychologist Naomi Eisenberger pursued this line of enquiry by studying the reactions of research participants' brains in a scanner while they played a virtual ball-tossing game. When the computer program excluded a participant from the game, their brains responded as they would have if they had been physically hurt. She sees this phenomenon as an illustration of our evolutionary past: we have developed to be together rather than alone, and to thrive best through inclusion and acceptance from others.

'I don't know if I've reached peak disappointment in Dad's eyes or not though.'

Jason looked down again, clearly wrestling with himself. I thought he was referring to his father's reaction to a potential move to Australia, but it took more time before I found out otherwise.

I didn't see Jason for a couple of weeks after we discussed his father's rejection. He cancelled each session at the last moment, apologetically, while dutifully assuring me that he'd paid me. It's not unusual for clients to regulate the intensity of their therapy by creating gaps in a weekly rhythm – it's a time-honoured pattern that doesn't suit everyone. I doubted that his absences were scheduling errors like his first one had been, and I wondered if he had backed away from our conversations because he had been stirred up – this time, the cigar was not just a cigar.

When he did return, he looked pale and exhausted, and he was less willing to look me in the eye. He was still in the habit of sitting down with his coat on, despite my encouragement to use one of the hooks behind my door. I wanted to talk about the impact of our meetings on him, as I was concerned that his dilemma had remained the same, but he was even more unhappy than when we first met. Therapy can do this sometimes. When we connect with feelings that we have safely tucked away it can become overwhelming, and if we have a self-critic lurking around, as I guessed Jason did, it might make itself known even more forcefully than before.

My first therapist used the metaphor of the Chinese finger puzzle game to describe the work of therapy. The puzzle looks like a small, simple woven bamboo cylinder. The idea is to put your finger into the opening at one end. The inside workings of the cylinder grip your finger, and most people's instinct is to pull their finger back towards their body in order to release it, but this causes the puzzle's hold to tighten. Counterintuitively, you need to push *into* the cylinder to release your finger, working against a fear of further entrapment.

In therapy, if all goes well, we are similarly released if we push into what we are fearful of, and the experience is almost never as bad as we anticipate. The author Michael Rosen described this process beautifully in his allegorical children's book *We're Going on a Bear Hunt*, in which a family sets off on an adventure but faces various obstacles, such as long grass, a cold river and mud: 'We can't go over it / We can't go under it. / Oh no! / We've got to go through it!'

Jason seemed to be both pushing and pulling, or not quite going through it. When he was present with me, I felt he was trying hard to engage but I also often felt disconnected from him and shut out, as if a part of him was sabotaging his honesty. Poised to ask if he had mixed feelings about coming to talk to me, given his absences, I realised that he had a more immediate problem he wanted to talk through and he launched into what was most on his mind.

'I'm stuck again!'

'Go on.'

'It's John's stag weekend and I'm supposed to be flying to Ibiza on Friday. I can't think of anything that I want to do less. I'm so busy and Kate and I need the time to talk.'

'What's so awful about your brother's stag party in Ibiza?'

I resisted the urge to add 'apart from the obvious'.

'I'm only invited because I'm his brother, and Dad won't go as it means leaving the country. We don't have cousins, so I'm the only family member going. He doesn't even like me that much! We are chalk and cheese. I can write the script of what will happen, and I'm not sure I can dig that deep to go through with it. It'll be hell on earth.'

'Can you give me any teasers from the script?'

'His best man will have got some enormous flashy villa, loads of people who I don't know will turn up to party, and we'll have to go clubbing both nights. John moves in a pack of lads, and if I don't keep up I'll be teased for being a poncy Londoner, and I won't be allowed to escape. And there'll also be lots of women about, and I don't want to see John behaving in ways his fiancée really wouldn't like. I've done my fair share of covering up for him.'

'How so?'

'At school he was always on the edge of trouble. Our school was tough and chaotic, and he had some pretty dodgy older mates who would deal drugs and steal cars. He had kudos for his football so he didn't have to prove himself by joining in too much. But if Dad had known John was anywhere near any of them, he would have gone ballistic. I'd often cover for him, even when I'd left home. Mum would call me, beside herself with worry.'

I couldn't imagine the diffident, thoughtful man sitting opposite me thriving at the school he described.

'How did you get on at school, then, was it tough and chaotic for you too?'

'I didn't enjoy it much. I turned up, kept my head down and then went to training at the end of the day. Like John, football kept me off the radar. I don't think I would have survived otherwise.'

'Was it a question of survival?'

'Kind of. It was pretty feral at times, and even the teachers struggled to cope. I wasn't a lad like most of the other boys in my year. I wasn't interested in petty crime, or drinking or drugs, and we couldn't have done any of that even if we had wanted to, as Dad would have kicked us off the team if he suspected anything. Being good at football was my acceptable pass.'

'Did you have friends?'

'A few. I was unusual for not treating girls like a separate species, and I hung out with them more. I am still very close to my best mate Millie – her cousin was the first person I stayed with in London. Millie's super smart and would help me out with studying – she's an academic now.'

'What did you need help with?'

'I wasn't very good at learning at school. I was interested in the lessons, but I struggled to keep up. It wasn't cool to care, but Millie did, and she knew that I did too. It was our dirty secret!'

I was surprised to hear that Jason hadn't learned with ease, even though I knew he hadn't achieved highly academically. He struck me as very clever, and when he spoke of his photography and work he was brilliantly articulate.

'What do you mean, "not very good at learning"?'

'I'm slow at processing information when it is taught to me, or if I have to read it quickly, and I really struggle with short-term memory for exams. I'm good at what I do now because I've learnt everything practically, on the job, and by watching what others do. I'm told I have a good eye too. Kate suspects I'm dyslexic, as she has had some training in it through her work.'

Undiagnosed dyslexia often crops up in my conversations with clients who felt inadequate at school. It's only relatively recently that teachers have been trained to spot it, even though it is thought at least one in ten of us live with it. Many still slip through the net, until it is caught in further or higher education, and others remain undiagnosed for a lifetime. Another client of mine, around Jason's age, described feeling as if she wore an invisible dunce's cap throughout her years in the classroom, and this shame continues to plague her.

'I have a better sense of your survival comment now. You didn't fit in with your peers, and you didn't have the right help with your learning.'

'I just felt stupid. Even the most disruptive kids would get things quicker than me. But I was good at English and history because they involved stories, and art. I tend to remember those well. It was why I loved film so much too.'

'Did you feel stupid everywhere?'

'If anything, I was the intellectual at home, and I would read books, even if I did so very slowly. Dad couldn't understand why Millie and I went to the cinema, or why I'd go to my room to read. Both my parents left school at sixteen – he was taught plumbing by my grandad, and Mum went to secretarial college. But I suspect Dad is dyslexic too: I've never seen him read a book and he gives all his paperwork to Mum to do. He never read us stories when we were young – he'd leave that to Mum or Gran.'

'Did your mum know about your struggles with lessons?'

Sadness flashed across Jason's face.

'I didn't ever want to bother her as she was always on the go. She bent her life around all of us and then she had Gran to look after too. She never had a day off as weekends were all about football.'

'So she was involved with the club too?'

'She still is. She runs the back end: ordering kit, equipment, sorting out the schedule for the season and getting sponsorship. She also helps Dad with his business and does loads for John too.'

'She sounds like a saint!'

'She is amazing. In my last season, our kits arrived without the sponsor's logo on. She drove through the night to pick the patches up and then spent the entire Friday and Saturday sewing them on by hand for a match on the Sunday. She was mortified when she spotted the odd wonky stitch and kept quiet about her calluses.'

Jason looked sad as he thought of his mum's selflessness.

'She'd do anything for anyone, and she's devoted to Dad, and he is to her in his own peculiar way. She used to pour his cereal into his bowl every morning, while we would do our own from an early age. It's not my style of relationship, but it seems to work for them. I worry that she doesn't look after herself, though, and I feel guilty that I've spread my wings and she never has.'

'She reminds me a little of how you describe Kate.'

'They are both selfless, that's true. Although Kate does look after herself far better, and I like to think I'm nothing like Dad. Kate is more her own person than Mum. And I'm not expecting her to do everything for me.'

Each time we spoke, I'd pick up on more clues as to why Jason could come down on himself so harshly: the imposition of his father's dream upon his own, his feeling stupid and out of sync with his peers at school, as well as his strong sense of rejection from his father and brother. Even his mother's tireless caregiving meant she had inadvertently overlooked his desires to be someone other than what was expected of him. There was enough for me to make sense of his internalised criticism, but there was far more to come.

Jason looked pretty shell-shocked when I saw him next, just a couple of days after his return from Ibiza. Though tempted to fabricate an excuse, he couldn't face the fall-out of not showing up for the stag party, guessing it would be yet another stick for John to beat him with.

'It was exactly as I told you it would be: John and his fifteen cronies partying non-stop, and a lot of chat that was meaningless to me – I'm just so different from that scene. I can talk good football, but it's a performance, really, and that's about the only topic I share with them. I felt like I was a jigsaw piece put in the wrong box.'

This was a familiar feeling for Jason and a theme of many of the conversations we'd had. He told me more about the stag weekend and his growing sense of isolation, boredom and dislike of his brother and his friends. He had salvaged some of this endurance test by hiring a car on one of the mornings to explore the hills and take photographs. But then his story ran out of steam and he dipped his head down to rest it in his hands again, a gesture of shame that I'd come to know.

'But there's something else that I think I should say. It's about time now. Only Millie knows, and she has urged me to tell you. She knows I've been talking to you.'

A heavy silence followed that perplexed me but also made me desperate to make things easier for him.

'I'm ready to hear you, but please take your time.'

Without looking up, he continued.

'I lied to you before, and I've been lying to lots of people for years. I do think Kate is gorgeous – anyone can see that. But the truth is I haven't ever really fancied her. She was keen to push things from a friendship into something more, and I thought the feelings would come, but they didn't. And they won't.'

I waited, knowing more was to come.

'I'm not sure that I am attracted to women at all – Kate or anyone else. I'm attracted to men. But I need more time to work this out. I can't go to Australia.'

He looked up and said what I imagined he'd rehearsed in his head many times.

'It hit me hard in Ibiza – that I can't go on hiding it any

more. There was a lot of pressure from John and his mates to hook up with women – "What happens on tour, stays on tour" crap. I couldn't even pretend to go along with it. And being with John again brought so much home to me.'

'Like what?'

'Like growing up pretending to be someone I wasn't. I wasn't a footballer, and now I have to accept that I'm never going to have the wife that is expected of me either, let alone one who pours my cereal out for me. John doesn't know the real me – he sees me as a posh older brother who abandoned his family for streets paved in gold. And we've discussed how Dad doesn't get me either. Neither would accept me if I came out.'

Jason's revelation surprised me, but it also made sense. I had often felt he was on the cusp of telling me something before backing away. His ambivalence about coming to see me reflected his internal conflict between wanting to be honest with himself, and with me, and his ongoing fears of doing so. A part of him still criticised his true self because he believed the many pejorative messages from the men of his childhood world, and of course the world we both inhabit now.

'How does it feel to have said that out loud?'

'Liberating and terrifying. Liberating because it's a fundamental truth about me that I have kept buried for too long. Terrifying because I don't think my family will take it well. I have a brother who calls me a ponce for living in London. My father believes in therapy to cure homosexuality. And Mum will be upset. She's sheltered and afraid of lots of things. She'll be scared for me.'

Jason was still looking down at his feet. I thought of how my own professional organisation does its utmost to distance itself from so-called conversion therapy and its egregious premise that homosexuality is a pathology. I assumed that he knew I found his brother's and father's prejudices abhorrent, but I couldn't be sure, so I stated it in unequivocal terms.

'I'm so sorry that your father and brother feel the way that they do. It isn't right, and you don't deserve that bigotry.'

I tried to encourage Jason to talk more, but he was too choked up and couldn't tolerate me looking at him. He moved on to his worries about his workload and left our session a few minutes before we were due to end. Not for the first time, he regulated his intense and difficult feelings by taking them away from the consulting room.

Jason didn't turn up for the following session, and unlike other times when he missed a meeting, I didn't hear from him beforehand. I left a message, asking him to call me back to talk on the phone, thinking that would be easier than a return to the more confronting space of my consulting room, but I didn't hear from him again.

I worried that Jason felt so terribly about himself – for being someone his father and brother would despise, for breaking Kate's heart, and for not ever feeling in sync with his surroundings – that he felt he didn't deserve therapy. Sometimes self-criticism, when it creates such a force of shame, is intractable: nothing or no one can initiate enough self-worth or self-compassion to work against it. I worried that I had mishandled our time together, and that I'd missed opportunities to help him ease up on himself. But I also held the hope that a rupture that isn't repaired doesn't always mean that the therapy preceding it wasn't helpful.

Early on in my training, I worked as a volunteer at a

university counselling service in London. Nervous with inexperience, I met with a young woman for an assessment, and clumsily worked my way through the list of questions on the standard form provided to me. There wasn't much time for other enquiries, nor any wise insights scraped from my veneer of expertise, but although she seemed to leave satisfied enough, she didn't return for the counselling that was subsequently offered to her.

Months later, I saw this student in a corridor on my way to the staff canteen for lunch. Her face lit up on seeing me, and she took me aside to thank me earnestly for our one-off session. I had, apparently, made her feel so much better by taking such care to listen to her, and had somehow given her strength to speak up to others and to risk being the person she really needed to be. It was possible that Jason felt something of the same, and that our conversations had at the very least given him a valuable opportunity to feel accepted for *all* of who he really was.

Chapter Five

Othering

Children know only themselves as reasons for
happenings in their lives. So of course as a child I
decided there must be something terribly wrong
with me that inspired such contempt.

AUDRE LORDE,
'Eye to Eye'

On my website, I refer to my earlier professional life as a
lawyer. Because of this disclosure, I have worked with a steady
trickle of solicitors, barristers and in-house lawyers over the
years, all of them drawn to the idea that I have some inkling
of the many stressors that come with the profession. Amanda
was one of them, emailing me at 2 a.m. one Saturday to tell me
that she desperately needed help with stress management. She
added that she was sending this message to me in tears, from
the back of a cab taking her home from the office.

We arranged to meet on a Monday at 9 p.m. This is my
latest regular evening appointment, and it has unwittingly

become my lawyer slot as it seems to be the only feasible time many can make a weekly commitment, although cancellations inevitably happen. Teachers tend to like late afternoons, after school; journalists usually go for early mornings before work; while the many freelancers are flexible and can see me at various times during the day. If I hadn't offered this late session time, I don't think Amanda would have made it to therapy at all.

People often create a ritual of arrival at my consulting room. Amanda established hers from the start: ringing the bell a few minutes late, then dealing with something on one of the two phones in her hand as I opened the door and beckoned her in. She'd then spend a few moments turning her phones to silent and placing her laptop, coat and enormous bag in the hallway outside my consulting room.

Various objects of aspiration rather than actual use would inevitably tumble out from her pile of things. I would find out how she never had the spare time to read the recently published book or wear the trainers at the gym, or even to choose a holiday from the glossy travel magazine. But carrying these things around gave her a sense of hope, even though she knew full well that it was fanciful – her job was too demanding.

When she eventually settled into one of my chairs for the first time, the energy of her arrival quickly dissipated. Facing a stranger in an unfamiliar room to talk about yourself is a big change of gear from a long day at any office, and many people don't know how to begin their therapy after reaching out to make an appointment. While silence in sessions can be fruitful, I won't let it be the start of an initial meeting: it can run the risk of making a prospective – and usually very vulnerable – client feel deeply uneasy, or at worst punished. So I took over.

'I understand from your email that you would like help with managing your stress. Can you tell me more about this?'

Amanda immediately covered her face with her hands.

'I'm sorry. I think I might cry.'

She took a deep breath, and didn't cry, and I suspected this wasn't the first time she'd suppressed her tears.

'I'm just having a really bad day. Yet another really bad day.'

'Finishing work this late seems bad enough, and I know you had had an incredibly long shift when you first emailed me. But I'm guessing that your long hours aren't all of the problem.'

'Ha! This is an early finish for me, although I will have to do some more work when I get home. You're right, though, the long hours aren't the problem.'

'What is?'

'Around this time last year, I moved to a different litigation team to work on a new case that the firm landed. My lovely boss, Sara, was leaving and she championed my move. It was supposed to be my chance to prove myself, so that I could be promoted from an assistant to a senior assistant. That's just not happening. In fact, I feel like I've gone backwards.'

Amanda had moved from a small law firm to a far larger and more prestigious one four years previously. For ambitious young lawyers like she seemed to be, this was an impressive achievement and a wise move, and I knew from my own brief time in the law that it would make her CV sparkle far more than it had. Amanda had already given her pound of flesh to the litigation department, with regular eighty-hour working weeks. Her social life had shrunk but she had enjoyed the intellectual challenges her fine mind needed to thrive, along with a growing bank balance.

'I don't mind working hard if I have the right people around me and the work is interesting. Sara had built a great team and she taught me so much, I loved working for her. But she's had a baby now and I doubt she'll come back – women rarely do after maternity leave. I miss her, as she'd be a support to me now.'

Hearing of the likely effect of Sara's new motherhood provoked strong feelings in me, but I needed to put aside my inclination to talk about discrimination against women in the workplace. Therapists are taught early on in their training to bracket – or leave aside – responses that are too personal, and it's a skill that many of us need to regularly revisit and sharpen.

'I was really excited to move teams at first, and ready to work just as hard. I knew I wasn't going to click with my new boss, as he's notorious for being difficult and demanding, and old school. Only a few people get on with him, so I knew not to take anything he said or did too personally. I moved on a high.'

'And now you feel so low. I'm so sorry.'

Amanda's tears began again, and this time she couldn't stop them. She spoke quickly through them, while taking tissues from the box on the table between us.

'I feel miserable all the time and I can't shift it. Work has gone from being a place I loved to a place I dread. The work I am doing now is more like the work I was doing years ago – small bits of advice, minute-taking and endless hand-holding of our client. The other assistant, James, gets all the work I should be doing, but he's no more qualified than me. I've gradually been pushed out. And I don't get on with the rest of the team.'

Taking a moment to blow her nose, she went on.

'But then I worry that I'm contributing to all of this as I'm not performing as well as I used to. I keep slipping up and making mistakes. So maybe I deserve the shitty work as I'm no longer a safe pair of hands.'

'Tell me about the rest of your team that you don't get on with?'

'Well, it's led by a man with a forensic brain but no people skills – as I said, I can more or less ignore him. Then there's a couple of senior – male – assistants who live on a different planet: they went to the same posh school and same university, and talk about stuff I honestly have no idea about. Then there's me and James. Either he doesn't see what's going on, or he chooses not to. There are also a couple of trainees and a couple of paralegals. I am supposed to be managing them but I'm not doing a very good job of it. I don't want any of them to see how crap I feel, and I know I'm being too hands-off.'

'But it sounds like you feel pushed out to the edge of where you should be – of course you feel crap.'

Amanda wiped her final tears as she broke out into a laugh.

'Even if I was given the work I should have, I'd still feel near the edge. Apart from one of the trainees and one of the paralegals, everyone else is a man. A white man.'

This depressing, almost inevitable comment really mattered, because it was freighted with so much that we needed to talk about early on in our work together: Amanda was a Black woman in a white and patriarchal world. I might have a pretty good idea of what it's like to be a woman, and I make it my business to readily detect even the subtlest of misogynies, but I can't ever, even remotely, know what it's like not to be white.

My whiteness brings innumerable privileges that mean I have lived a life of far greater psychological and physical safety than Amanda. I see myself reflected everywhere, and others see me as a part of their commonality. As Reni Eddo-Lodge powerfully states in her vital book *Why I'm No Longer Talking to White People About Race*, 'To be white is to be human; to be white is universal. I only know this because I'm not.' I needed to acknowledge this difference between Amanda and me, or else I ran the risk of suggesting that it wasn't as important as it was.

'It's my job to understand what it feels like to be you as best I can. If we carry on meeting, I want to acknowledge that I only know what it's like to be white and I will have to work harder to know what your lived experience is like. We share our gender and I know a bit about being a solicitor to begin with, but not what has come from the colour of your skin.'

I deeply regret that I wouldn't have named this difference – or indeed other differences – when I began practising nearly twenty years ago. My professional training lacked adequate depth when it came to thinking about historical and systemic racism, along with its impact on the psychological work in the consulting room. It also didn't think enough about the fact that people from non-white backgrounds are significantly under-represented in psychological professions, which remains true today, as does a continuing inadequacy of training around racial and cultural difference in mental health settings.

When I was training, I was encouraged to spend time studying and thinking about the transmission of traumas from genocides and wars down the generations, but barely anything was mentioned about the transmission of the traumas of enslavement, caste systems and colonialism. I do think about that now, far too late in the day to have given justice to so many of my past clients. But while my shame has no place in the consulting room, my duty to be educated does, as does my duty to talk about what I learn.

'To be honest, I wanted to work with a Black therapist, but I couldn't find one near me, or one who could see me so late in an evening. And I liked the fact you were an ex-lawyer.'

I was the best Amanda could do, and with the soothing words of Winnicott in mind, I could only try to be good enough.

Amanda's firm had an employee assistance programme which offered short-term counselling support. Its underlying premise was to get the employee back to work as soon as possible, rather than launching a deeper and longer enquiry into the cause of any distress. Although she could access this confidentially, Amanda wasn't the first client I have met who preferred to avoid any risk of mental ill-health leaking out to an employer. So she paid for me privately and kept quiet about her need to leave 'early' on a Monday night. Even though employers are increasingly awakening to the importance, and justice, of caring for their employees' mental health, I regularly discover that many haven't made any real efforts towards this.

I first met Amanda when Covid-19 began to permeate our consciousness from the reports coming out of Wuhan. Therapy never happens in a vacuum and the distress of national and global problems will often be noted before sessions truly begin. We referred to the horrors of the (then) epidemic, with the false safety of believing it would remain sequestered, thousands of miles away from our island nation. At this point we also naïvely assured ourselves that it was just a nasty flu that could be contained with a bit of distance and eager handwashing.

Amanda had little bandwidth to worry about a potential pandemic at this time. She was feeling increasingly despondent about her role, and I found out more about how she had been led to believe it was something different from what it had turned out to be. She had been assured by her awkward new boss on their first meeting that she could hone her established and respected skills as a litigator as well as expanding them by managing the small team of trainees and paralegals.

'I was recruited to do something that I've then been blocked from doing. It's ridiculous. When I first met my new boss, he said he needed a "feisty" team member on board, like me. You wouldn't know it! I'm a glorified secretary and nanny now.'

I couldn't help a sharp intake of breath on hearing this. Feisty as a descriptor for a woman is guaranteed to wind me up. I tend to interpret it as a comment about someone behaving in a way that women aren't supposed or expected to behave, and my mind leaps to Prime Minister David Cameron telling a female MP to 'calm down, dear' from the despatch box. Nor have I ever heard the word used to describe a man; the same is true for other gendered words such as shrill, hysterical and fierce.

Amanda smiled in recognition at my inhalation.

'Honestly, it doesn't even bother me any more. I have heard it so many times over the years – at school, at university, at law school, at my last firm. I'm the one with a quick tongue or the one to be wary of. I even had a tutor at university who told the lecture hall to "give me a wide berth" in debates. I think he thought he was flattering me somehow, or I like to think that.'

'Yes, it makes me wonder if he'd say the same to a male student.'

'Of course not, nor would he have said it if I were white. You'll never be feisty in the way that I can be. A feisty Black woman is also aggressive and to be feared.'

I know of that stereotype well, of course, and have reflected upon my own unbidden fear of Black women's anger. I would have to be brain dead not to be affected by this culturally created bias, however hard I resist and resent it. I wish I could claim this fear didn't stir inside of me still, but it does, and I strive to be vigilant of its existence. Only then can I do my very best to challenge it and put it aside. This makes for a sticky realm of self-criticism in me – even though unconscious biases are beyond my control, I can't help berating myself for the fact I have them.

Amanda spent the first few sessions letting off steam about how sidelined she had become, and how powerless she felt in the face of her effective demotion. She had three close female friends who had their own problems to contend with, and she didn't want to burden them with this ongoing story. Her mother, her closest relative, 'was a long story we need more time for', and I suspected she was linked to Amanda's desire to be so guarded with both friends and family. But I also got to know more about her life in a world that favoured people like me.

'Does a fish know the ocean exists? I have always lived as a minority that is seen as inferior to the rest. I don't know any different. I stood out from almost all of the girls at the school I went to, and then again at university, and at law school. I'm now working in a firm where most of the fee-earners are white. Most of the Black employees are legal secretaries, the security guards, a receptionist and, more recently, a few train-ees. I have even wondered if I was recruited to tick a diversity box, rather than for my actual skills.'

I couldn't know if this comment sprung from a dismal truth, or from Amanda's plunging self-worth. Her self-criticism was an understandable response to all that she had told me about her work situation so far, but it also had to be connected with the systemic 'inferiority' that she was born into. Simone de Beauvoir wrote, in her famous work *The Second Sex*, 'When an individual (or a group of individuals) is kept in a situation of inferiority, the fact is that he is inferior.' I wanted to know when Amanda first realised this harsh reality, guessing it was a moment that marked the beginning of many traumas.

'I don't remember much before I went to school. My mum came over from Ghana when she was pregnant with me and moved in with my auntie and my uncle and their young kids. I'm still really close to my cousins, and my auntie is like a second mum. But she moved back to Ghana with my uncle, so I don't see her so much any more.'

Amanda's father had been much older than her mother and had died of a heart attack just five months after she was conceived. Floored by grief, her mother came to England to join her sister. Amanda had grown up knowing how clever, successful and kind her father was, and his memory lived on a high pedestal that her mother clearly wanted Amanda to occupy too. I wasn't surprised to hear that he had been a litigation lawyer as well.

'I think it was when I first went to school that it really hit me that I wasn't the same as many others. We had moved out of my auntie's by then to a different area, so I wasn't at school with my cousins. I must have been five as I was in reception, standing with my back against the wall in the playground watching others play. A girl stood next to me. She didn't say anything, but picked up my arm with both of her hands and stroked my skin a few times. She then dropped my arm and ran back to play. I remember that moment so well, because up until then, I hadn't thought that I was any different from her, or the others.'

'At the risk of asking a stupid question, how did that make you feel?'

Amanda chuckled, as if to agree with my stupidity.

'Rejected. And – suddenly – really shit about myself. I didn't know whether I should go and play or not. I was stuck against that wall, watching all the white girls playing together. I suddenly hated them, and I wanted to run away but I couldn't.'

Amanda's frown and flushed skin signalled the return of her humiliation and anger from all the years before and I knew that it was a trauma that had been repeated. I pushed my feet into the floor as a means to quell my deep discomfort at what I was hearing, but also my regret at not speaking more about this to other clients of colour.

'Did you tell your mum?'

'I did, and I remember the sadness on her face – she doesn't show it often. She then quickly hardened up and gave me a lecture that I would hear over and again. About the fact I would have to work far harder than white people to get anywhere, and that I shouldn't trust white people to be on my side. That we'd be forever made to feel different, and criticised.'

I nodded, wanting to protest with assurances of my own trustworthiness. But I also knew my implicit bias worked against this.

Amanda carried on, and her anger dissipated as quickly as it had arrived.

'I didn't want to believe her, but I *have* had to graft and I have felt different. I worked really hard to get a scholarship to a private school and it paid half my fees. I was the only Black girl in my class, but also, I was the only girl to have a single parent. My home life was completely different from most of the girls around me – they had big houses, and some had weekend homes, and they'd have ski holidays at half term. They'd barely heard of Ghana!

'My friends were the "poor ones" who had just one house and may have gone away once in the summer. Mum did so well to pay the mortgage and the rest of my school fees. She worked her fingers to the bone. She still does, even though she doesn't need to any more.'

As we tried to disentangle all the threads that led to Amanda's feelings of low self-worth, I knew from previous comments that one was tied to her relationship with her mother. They were close, messaging each other most days, but Amanda often alluded to her mother's exhausting desire for her to prove herself professionally. She would often laugh this off, but I could sense how tiring – and effective – this pressure actually was. One evening, she sat down and immediately started shaking her head from side to side. My opportunity to learn more about her mother had arrived.

'Well, I'm in big trouble for seeing you!'

'In your opinion or someone else's?'

By this time, we were both familiar with Amanda's

self-sabotaging self-talk: it leaked through all her narratives and she regularly convinced herself not to speak up at work for fear of outing herself as a failure. She also berated her body and appearance, and gave them to me as reasons not to date. I wondered if she might have been referring to her sessions in my consulting room, given the fears of transmission of the virus that were then on everyone's lips. I too had begun to doubt the safety of seeing clients in person, and knew I had to address this matter very soon.

'Well, as you know, on Saturday I went home, for Mum's birthday party, for the first time in a very long time. Maybe it's the last gathering we'll have for a while if we do get locked down. I thought I was doing my best to be happy and carefree, but she always wants to know that things are going well at work. She wants my promotion more than me. But she knew something was up as I have been messaging her less often, and slow to reply to her messages, and she could tell my reassurances were fake. She knows me far too well. I sometimes think she loves me too much! So I ended up telling her that the move to the team hadn't worked out as I'd hoped and that I'd been really stressed.'

I raised my eyebrows in anticipation of her mum's response.

'I knew this would freak her out, but I couldn't lie to her any more. Sure enough, she went off on one before I had a chance to explain anything.'

'Meaning?'

'She accused me of being careless and assumed I'd been "mouthy" again – she always assumes I'm the cause of my problems. I've lost count of the times I've said to her, "It's not my fault." She even said I pay too much attention to my social life. As if I had time! I've barely seen my friends for months.'

'She sounds really worried for your financial stability, perhaps like she has been for her own. She only had herself to rely on to look after you.'

'I know. But she never takes my side. If my auntie had been there, she would have stepped in to calm her down. Even when I was at school, I could never complain to my mum about a teacher as she would have made it all about me doing something wrong. She would always say "just keep your head down, don't cause trouble and do well".'

'Is that what got her through life? Keeping her head down and doing well?'

'I'm sure it was. Her mantra, as you know, was that I'd have to work twice as hard to get half as far as anyone else – anyone white, that is. She had two, sometimes three jobs to get her through university when she arrived. She had worked for my dad's law firm in Ghana in the accounts department, and when she arrived here and decided to settle she retrained as an accountant. She runs her own business now and refuses to retire, even though she's paid off her mortgage.'

Amanda's mother had clearly set the bar high, but living up to the successes of a dead parent can also be a source of ongoing pressure. The frequent consequence of such a silent pressure is a tendency to criticise ourselves if we don't reach the heady heights it is pushing us towards.

'You have two impressive role models to live up to.'

'I had to do well. There was no other option. And nothing can get in the way of that – even if I'm feeling crap.'

'So when you explained how unhappy you were, she still freaked out?'

Amanda laughed again.

'Don't get me wrong, because my mum is an amazing

woman and I respect her so much. But she worries far more about what other people think than what she, or I, may be feeling. She tuts if I cry!'

'She doesn't want to talk about things that are upsetting.'

'Nope. She doesn't see the point of it, but I know it's also because she doesn't want me to be upset. She buries things so deep – her grief for Dad's death, her loneliness raising me, her homesickness for Ghana. And the racism – I've been through nothing compared to her. My auntie is more open than her, and she's told me how hard it was when they both settled over here.'

'She has suffered so much trauma,' I ventured. 'Many of us cope with that by denying our pain, and then we can get into the habit of denying any other vulnerability too. I wonder if your mum coped that way when she came to England as a widow, with much of the world against her. She dug deep and proved to everyone she could manage just fine.'

If I was right that Amanda's mum had protected herself from her own trauma in this way, it also meant that she had perhaps unconsciously passed this on to Amanda. This buried trauma would also carry historical and cultural traumas of generations before her. Academics have studied transgenerational trauma since the mid-sixties, first amongst the children of Holocaust survivors, and subsequently amongst children and grandchildren of many others such as African Americans and survivors of the Khmer Rouge atrocities of Cambodia and the Rwandan genocide.

We can pass on the profound impact of trauma through things said, such as the repeated message to Amanda that the world wasn't truly safe or accepting of her, and that she'd have to work so hard to flourish rather than rely upon help.

We can also transmit our pain through things not said, which can leave a child confused because she knows without having been told that her parent's pain exists in the silence. In more recent years, researchers have even found associations between ancestral trauma and epigenetic changes (environmentally driven molecular processes that turn genes on and off), which suggest we carry the pain of previous generations in our cells.

'I'm still curious as to why you are in big trouble for seeing me today.'

'I ended up telling my mum I was in therapy and she hit the roof. She cannot bear to think of me telling anyone about my private life. I was always told to mind my own business and to keep my own business to myself. I think she did open up to Dad, but then her grief, and her experiences coming here, sealed her heart up. So that's why I'm in trouble. But it's always a storm in a teacup with Mum. We're all right really.'

Not long after this session, Covid-19 became a major domestic threat and we were unable to meet in my consulting room. Stuck in our homes, we were swamped by a tsunami of shock, fear, grief and the unbearableness of not knowing what the immediate and further future held. We crave knowledge that will help us control our lives and contain our anxieties, but in the early stages of the pandemic we knew next to nothing about the impact of the virus on the human body, how it was transmitted, nor for how long we would need to suspend our lives. Amanda and I were in it together, but I had to work hard at bracketing my own turmoil so that it wouldn't intrude on our weekly hour together.

Amanda was happy to meet online because, like many of us, much of her professional and social life had migrated in the same way. She was understandably fearful and we didn't know at this stage that communities of colour would be affected much more harshly. She and her mother both lived alone and they decided to keep it that way rather than quickly creating a household together as some single people did.

'I can't work with Mum around – her iron rod would finish me off! Plus, she doesn't even want me at hers, as that would be admitting a need for support. We're good on Zoom. And I'm scared of giving her the virus as I'm going to the shops every day. I'd never forgive myself.'

Without having to rush to my consulting room from her office, Amanda was able to call me on time, and was ready to talk, so our sessions gained another ten minutes. We could also meet earlier in the evening, as both of our diaries were reorganised. The time she saved from not having her daily commute was also a gift to her stress levels, along with the physical distance she now had from undermining personalities at work.

'I didn't actually realise how much energy it took just to be in the same room as the others, especially James. It was so humiliating watching him fly while my own wings felt clipped. I now realise how much I didn't want to be there, and how often I wanted to cry. At least at home I don't have to share a space with him, or any of them. I am sleeping better, and for longer. It's odd because in some ways I do feel more relaxed.'

I found that many other clients, despite their fears and grief for so many losses brought on by the pandemic, also benefited from an enforced slower pace of life. Many spoke of having more time and mental space, and this allowed some to reflect on their lives in new ways – at least those still in employment, or on furlough, and so with some financial stability. Amanda confronted her self-critic more and more, recognising how much it had influenced her and pushed her hard to achieve.

'I have been thinking about how my ambition has been steered by what I believed the world thought of me. Not feeling good enough made me want to prove myself. It's not just Mum's pushiness. I understand how her own experience of feeling so much worse than the rest meant she wanted me to be better than the rest. And she wants me to reflect Dad's glory.'

As she wedged a little more space between her self-critic and her observer self, Amanda was also better able to connect with what she really wanted from work.

'I don't think I want to get het up about breaches of commercial contracts for faceless corporate companies. I want to do well, but I care about other things more.'

I was talking to many people at that time about their desire to focus more on what they realised to be more important: family, friends, community and health – and politics. Then, a couple of months into lockdown, another historically ignored pandemic came to light: systemic racism. Yet another Black person, George Floyd, was brutally murdered by a police officer, and the world ignited in protest.

When Amanda and I met a few days after this atrocity, she looked completely exhausted and distracted, and I was careful to keep my own feelings away from our conversation. I knew that she had to have been thinking about, and re-experiencing, the repeated traumas of racism towards her and others. After a few seconds, I named what I felt to be there between us.

'I'm thinking that George Floyd's murder brings up a lot for you.'

Amanda nodded and then smiled weakly in a bid to hold it together. She told me of her plans to join with friends and thousands of others to walk the streets of London as part of the Black Lives Matter protest. She showed me a box that she had found outside her local shop which she would be using to make a placard.

'If it feels okay to talk about it now, I want to know more about your own experiences that you will also march for.'

Amanda looked away from the camera and spoke far more softly than usual. I had to strain to hear.

'Do you want the obvious stuff or the less obvious?'

'Both. But please start where you want to.'

'I've told you about that time in primary school. I've had racist abuse thrown at me loads of times. Some of it really sticks – like once at a bus stop when I was on my own, and another time when I was leaving a club with friends. It's pretty standard that I will be asked where I come from when I meet new people, especially outside London. I'll say London. And it'll be, "No, no, where are you really from?" As if I'm the one to have got it wrong! It all adds up. No wonder I can feel I get things wrong.'

Amanda mostly looked away from the camera as she spoke and I felt torn between wanting her to tell me more and not wanting to upset her further. She left a long silence, that I broke when I guessed it to be right.

'And the less obvious stuff?'

'The list is long: people assuming I have a good singing voice – like at work, someone I have never met emailed me to ask if I wanted to join the office choir. Or that I'm physically strong and good at sport.'

Now looking at me and holding a handful of her braids, she

said, 'But the thing that really gets me is that my hair seems to be an exotic artefact available for others to comment on, and even touch.'

'How do you deal with all of this?'

'I have had to learn to choose my battles. I can't let myself get angry each and every time, or I'll have nothing left. But I have never protested for Black Lives Matter before and I'm looking forward to getting angry then. Being with others will help. I can't tell Mum, though, as I know she'll worry about me.'

It is a well-accepted idea among some therapeutic circles that certain depressions – whether clinically diagnosed or not – are fuelled by an anger that has collapsed and turned inward. In Freud's seminal work *Mourning and Melancholia* (1917) he distinguished these two psychological phenomena from one another – in mourning anger is directed towards the lost love while in melancholia anger becomes a form of self-attack.

Many decades later, the early theorists of cognitive behavioural therapy (CBT), the talking therapy favoured by the National Health Service, also correlated depression with an anger turned against oneself. It often feels far too risky to show anger towards a more powerful person or people, so it becomes safer to direct that force against ourselves instead.

It was good to hear that Amanda wasn't collapsing her anger inwards again, and the protests made me think of the notion of 'fierce compassion' described by the US academic and author Kristin Neff. She describes how compassion, aimed at alleviating the suffering of others as well as of ourselves, is typically thought of as tender but can be 'ferocious' too (like a bear protecting her cub). Culturally prescribed gender roles prefer women to act out the former version, while men gain kudos for the latter. But Neff makes a call for women, in particular, to embrace both: 'The boat needs to be rocked. When we hold our pain with fierce-empowered-truth we can speak up and tell our stories . . . we need to do so if we are going to effectively stand up to patriarchy, to racism, and the people in power that are destroying our planet.'

Our conversations during lockdown taught me far more about the alienation Amanda had always felt, and how, in turn, this had caused her to unwittingly join others in putting herself down. She had been stirred up by recent events, though, and energised to make a change.

In the weeks that followed the global protests, people became more aware of and educated about systemic racism and prejudice. Reni Eddo-Lodge's book became a bestseller again, along with many others such as Layla Saad's *Me and White Supremacy* and Robin DiAngelo's *White Fragility*. Broadcast media rescheduled their programming to air topical documentaries and films, and interviews about racial injustice with influential thinkers and activists. Protestors in Bristol threw a statue of Edward Colston, a slave trader, into the harbour. As a child, I had loved visiting friends in this city, knowing nothing of how its wealth had flowered.

Many organisations publicly pledged their commitment to anti-racist policies and my own profession, the United Kingdom Council for Psychotherapy, responded with an acknowledgement of the 'festering wound of centuries-long racism', calling for training organisations to address the many barriers to accessing and completing training 'to ensure BAME therapists are entering the profession in greater numbers. Regardless of background, we must ensure all therapists have the cultural competence to meet clients and service users where they are.'

In the weeks following the protests, and as lockdown eased a little, Amanda became increasingly certain that she wanted to change professional tack and she began to focus on leaving her job. We began to meet in the longer lunch hour she gave herself, sometimes as she sat under the shade of a tree in a nearby park.

'I honestly don't know why I'm at most of the meetings at work these days. No one asks my opinion on anything any more, and when I do talk, James will often interrupt and take over, as if he's managing me. Our videoconferencing software is set up so that whenever someone starts talking, their face takes up the whole screen, and it's nearly always his or another similar-looking face filling it. It's just made things I knew already far more obvious.'

As she described this scene, I noticed how sanguine she sounded, as opposed to her previous emotion-choked stories. In the brilliant novel *Fleishman is in Trouble* by Taffy Brodesser-Akner, the narrator Libby reflects on her working life as a journalist on a men's magazine, describing it as 'like a woman in the world – unwelcome, auxiliary at best, there to fill in the rough spots that men don't want to'. As Amanda felt less defeated, she became less willing to fill in the rough spots.

By now our sessions had been reset to a slower pace, and she took time to tell me more about her dream to align her talents and desire for challenge in a direction that 'worked for people rather than faceless corporations'. She made this commitment more binding by talking it over with her friends, and even contacting a recruitment consultant. This also told me that her self-critic was in the way less and less, as otherwise it would have never let her have that small measure of confidence.

One week Amanda called, beaming and waving a bottle of beer at the camera.

'It's early for a beer for you, isn't it? Are you celebrating?'

'I can't believe this has happened given all we've been talking about.'

Amanda laughed in a slightly despairing way.

'You aren't laughing about something funny?'

'Hardly. I've been asked to chair a new diversity and inclusion committee at work. I predicted this would happen – I told my friends it wouldn't take long.'

'And this is a cause for celebration?'

'I know I have valuable insight that so many others don't and that could be good for the organisation. But I also have had so much valuable insight that has been ignored for so long now. I'm bearing a grudge that I don't want to let go of. The committee feels tokenistic and it can jog on.'

Amanda was still smiling.

'So what are you toasting, then? I'm now confused!'

'And then an hour after that email, Sara calls me. She had emailed me last week to say she was going to, but I didn't think much about it. She's setting up a small legal consultancy to specialise in representing women who have experienced discrimination in the workplace. She has guaranteed funding for a role she wants me to take up.'

'And you are?'

'Too right! And as long as I tell Mum that this new job means I've had a big promotion, she'll be happy enough.'

Amanda resigned a couple of weeks later. We continued to meet through the two months of her notice period and then the pandemic's first wave died down enough for us to say our goodbyes back in my consulting room, at a safe and sanitised distance. We awkwardly laughed as we bumped our elbows at the doorstep.

I had every hope that Amanda's new job would build upon her newly found confidence in herself, and that in turn this would provide a buffer against the forces that would try to put her down.

Chapter Six

Three not Two

There is still a strong tendency to view childlessness in a woman as a failure. A woman without children tends to receive either pity or rebuke.

ÉLISABETH BADINTER,
The Conflict

It was immediately obvious how at ease Helen and Nick were with each other by the way they made their way to my sofa. They seemed to read each other's minds about who would walk ahead and then who would sit where, and unlike many couples who ask for my help, they were holding hands when I greeted them at my door. They weren't in crisis or unable to communicate well, but they were serious about tending to their relationship, which needed some extra help and support as they faced what seemed to be their last attempt to conceive a child.

Helen had emailed me because I have an expertise in working with infertility and pregnancy loss. I find this a particularly exhausting area of my practice, despite many years of experience. Clients tend to seek me when they are already saturated with despair, feeling a type of grief that is the bottom rung of our cultural pecking order of loss. Unlike the work I do with clients experiencing non-chronic depression or anxiety, where I have hope about the direction of travel, I can't feel the same about protracted reproductive loss.

I've lost count of the times I have sat with a bereaved woman or couple who want me to reassure them they will become parents – something I can't do, even if the statistics are in their favour. I know of many psychological interventions – evidence based or otherwise – that alleviate the symptoms of anxiety or help lift a mood. But when it comes to infertility and pregnancy loss, I cannot be so confident of a positive outcome; there is too much not knowing, around both causes and potential treatments. The loss of five babies to miscarriage has also been of great personal pain to me, and I remain vigilant for the occasional intrusion of my own responses into other people's stories of similar loss.

Taking Nick's hand and looking at him before turning to me, Helen spoke first.

'We have been trying to conceive for over five years now, and I think we are beginning to buckle under the strain. We used to work well as a tag team, and if one of us was down, the other was up. But I've become really anxious, and I'd say Nick is depressed. I've never known him to be this low.'

Nick nodded and Helen then squeezed his hand as a signal for him to take over.

'I usually spring out of bed in the morning, but recently I just want to stay put. I'm exhausted all the time, and I have lost my mojo with everything. But we are here because we want to give a pregnancy one more shot, and we both want to feel a bit better before we do.'

Looking at Nick, Helen added, 'Also, I want to say in front of someone else that you have supported me so much, and I am so grateful. But I worry that I've been a burden for you, and I wish you would lean on others a bit more. Especially lately, with everything going on with my dad.'

When I meet couples, I often ask them to look at and speak to each other rather than speak *about* the other to me. Helen and Nick needed no encouragement from me to do this, though, as they weren't in conflict, and at no point needed to appeal to my mediation skills or imagined side-taking. Helen turned back to me to explain further.

'My dad was diagnosed with cancer eighteen months ago. He's had some pretty brutal treatment, and all is well for now. But it isn't a good one in terms of the long-term prognosis, and we can only hope he's in remission for years rather than weeks or months. I know how happy he would be to meet my child, and I am desperate to give him that. I feel so guilty that I haven't been there for him enough lately, because I've been so caught up with my own troubles.'

It was unsurprising to me to hear her criticising herself in the midst of so much grief, but at this stage, I had little idea of how far and deep this trait of hers ran.

Nick stroked Helen's hand as she began to cry, then replied.

'I feel like I'm letting you down, though, Hels. I'm supposed to be the one who sees the glass half full. I hate it that you have to go through so much with all our fertility stuff along with all the worry with your dad. I don't have to inject myself and take fake hormones and feel exhausted and bruised. I'm no good to you when I'm like this.'

Many men express remorse at not being good enough for their partner as they go through fertility struggles, even when they are suffering greatly too. Female partners say the same, of course, but men are still under the spell of a socially prescribed duty to be stoic and strong, protective and supportive. High-profile figures like Prince William are helpfully nudging along the idea that men can be – and need to be – emotionally vulnerable, but stereotyped ideas persist, especially in the reproductive realm, where a woman's body has to take centre stage.

As I committed to support the couple through one more round of fertility treatment, I had to remember Helen's grief for her father's anticipated death. Sometimes couples work has to shift focus to the stories of one partner for a while and may even run alongside their own individual therapy. But first I wanted to know more about their joint story of their imagined future family. This often begins a long time before a couple have actually begun to try to conceive.

Couples like Helen and Nick usually have little opportunity to speak about their fertility journey – a hackneyed phrase that euphemistically sums up an often lengthy and gruelling episode of life. They may well find solidarity with the 'one in six couples' statistic of infertility, but others in the same situation often have to be sought out and may well be strangers found online. The easiest part of my work with reproductive loss involves using my genuine curiosity – fed by my own experiences of pregnancy loss – to hear the beginning, middle and ongoing-ness of such narratives, asking about the details that others usually don't.

'Can you tell me about when you first decided to become parents? It doesn't matter who goes first.'

Helen spoke up quickly, as I'd expected her to. Women tend to talk about their dreams of motherhood with their friends and with themselves and may even have started to do so in the playground, as a young child. Men speak out loud of their desire for fatherhood far less, and boys rarely do so.

'When we first met, I was upfront about how I wanted kids. It was a deal-breaker for me. I couldn't be with someone who didn't want a child.'

She smiled at Nick. 'Luckily you were keen too! But we planned to wait until we were able to buy a flat, and then I got a new teaching job and I had to wait a year to establish my full maternity package. Then, five years ago this week in fact, we moved into our flat and began trying to conceive the following month. I kick myself now, of course, because I was thirty-three by then. I shouldn't have cared about the maternity leave and thought more about my fertility.'

I wasn't surprised to hear Helen blame herself for her struggle to conceive. Reproductive loss is nearly always bound up with self-recrimination and 'kicking myself' is a mild insult compared to other things I hear people say. I also recognised the precision of her memory when it came to the start of their efforts to make a baby. We remember dates that matter to us – birthdays, anniversaries, deaths – so it makes sense that we know those that mark the first step towards creating a much-wanted child. I often hear of the month, if not the exact day, when a couple stopped using contraception, and when conception occurred.

'For the first six months of trying we were quite relaxed, as we didn't expect to get pregnant instantly. But then we became less and less relaxed, and by the end of the year I was checking my temperature and using ovulation trackers. Meanwhile, everyone we know was getting pregnant or having babies, and we felt increasingly left behind. Baby showers became excruciating. In fact, I couldn't even look at the baby section in the supermarket without wanting to cry.'

'I wonder if you both feel envy towards these friends of yours.' I felt I could suggest this based on personal experience and many other clients' stories.

Helen and Nick looked at each other in recognition and both nodded.

Helen continued: 'I was, and am, genuinely delighted and happy for other people. But yes, I also find it really difficult each time I hear a pregnancy announcement – especially if it's unplanned. For some people, making a baby is like falling off a log and it reminds me that my body can't do what it is supposed to do. And then I hate myself for not being able to *just* feel delighted – I shouldn't taint it with my feelings of resentment.'

Another example of self-criticism had revealed itself. The couple then took turns to describe their repeated months of dashed hopes, and how the arrival of Helen's bleeding ushered in a mounting disappointment and sadness as well as a growing fear of their never conceiving at all. I heard how their efforts became all-consuming: their diet became complicated as they tried to eat apparently fertility-boosting foods, and their lifestyle more restrictive – no more long bike rides for Nick, for fear of reduced blood flow affecting his sperm production. Helen also reduced her commitments at work in an effort to reduce her day-to-day stress levels.

While their lives adapted in this strained way, they bore losses that were profound, complicated and hard to articulate: time to conceive, confidence in their bodies to create a pregnancy, the opportunity to join their peer group, and the innocence with which they began their joint dream. They also lost their child in their minds.

I said, 'Each month you lose the baby you shared in your imaginations, along with the myriad hopes and dreams of your future family life. Few can understand the weight of this tremendous loss, and I know that your grief is real, even if your baby had yet to be conceived.'

Helen nodded and looked at Nick again.

'We tried about twenty times to make a baby naturally before we gave up. That's a lot of times. It's true, we felt our imagined baby was crawling away from us. So we went to the GP who referred us to our nearest NHS fertility clinic. We had all the usual investigations, but our infertility is unexplained – we both tick all the boxes that we should. It's a double-edged sword: a relief not to have anything obviously wrong, but frustrating not having a solid reason why.'

Reproductive science can only take a desperate couple so far, and indeed it often provides only a few answers to the questions couples have. Its best expertise can't guarantee a conception, nor prevent or explain every miscarriage or still-birth, nor can it give adequate psychological support to those very many bereaved people who need it. I do my best with the last, but the support I offer people isn't free. Helen and Nick were just about able to pay; many others can't.

Nick looked at Helen and said something it felt like he'd said before.

'We became members of a club that we never signed up for.'

When Nick and Helen returned, I learned more about why their wished-for pregnancy would be their final attempt – or at least their last 'for now'. When they were referred to the clinic, they had been offered two cycles of IVF. Despite clear NHS policy recommendations to offer three cycles, the dreadful postcode lottery, which makes eligibility for infertility treatment so variable throughout the country, had played out less favourably for them. Many other couples are also offered only two cycles, or one, or even none at all.

Given that the IVF process means that a woman's body has to be treated with synthetic hormones, and then undergoes an invasive egg collection and a subsequent embryo transfer, it made sense that Helen took up the story.

'In the first round, I didn't respond to the drugs very well. My follicles didn't grow enough, and they couldn't collect any eggs. Or rather, I had "failed to respond".'

She gave a hollow laugh.

'As if I'd been lazy about the whole thing!'

'That's what you were told?'

'Yup! When we went back to the clinic to discuss what had happened, we met a new doctor. As he sat down, holding our file which he clearly hadn't read, he barely looked at me before saying "So, you are the lady who failed to respond!" He then went on to muse out loud about whether I had "ovarian failure", and how I might be a candidate for donor eggs. This is before he'd even opened my file. I now know that he was talking rubbish, but it was absolutely gutting to hear at the time, and it made me feel even more shit about myself.'

Given how frequently I hear it, I should be less affected by the language of failure peppering stories of infertility, but it still makes my heart sink and my blood boil. Pejorative words litter the written texts and spoken words of gynaecological and obstetric care – which means they are directed at the female body. While Helen's ovaries had been carelessly cast as 'failures', other women are told that they have 'failed to conceive or progress a pregnancy'. In the early times of my own many 'failures' twenty years ago, a female body could house an 'inhospitable womb', while her cervix produced 'hostile mucus'. My first, and very late, miscarriage was due to my 'incompetent cervix', and the birth of my youngest son at thirty-seven years of age made me 'geriatric'.

To be fair, appeals by charity and patient advocates to replace such derogatory descriptors are being listened to, but progress isn't fast enough, and I regularly hear stories from women like Helen who feel crushed by them. They nearly always intensify a pre-existing sense of inadequacy and self-criticism too, as Helen went on to explain.

'After that consultation I began to feel like I'd really let Nick, and everyone else, down. Dad was so excited about the IVF and was convinced we'd strike gold first go. I hated to hear the disappointment in his voice – I know he was sad for me, but it felt like a rehash of the many times I've let him down.'

Nick squeezed Helen's hand and took over. He clearly resisted her persistent self-reproach.

'Whatever grudge we both hold against the doctor for his sloppy words, we are grateful that he did let us try again. The clinic could have refused on the basis of Helen's non-response. We did the next cycle with a different drug regime and Helen produced lots of follicles – and the first attempt didn't count towards our allotted two. We collected five eggs, and three embryos were made. We called them the three amigos but only one was good enough for transfer.'

Nick paused, but of course I already knew what was coming.

'It didn't work. It was excruciating as it was the closest that we'd come to actually getting pregnant, or at least to our knowledge. We had so much hope.'

It's surprising to many people that an IVF loss can hit just as hard as a loss in an established pregnancy. The bond with an unborn child – who may be just an 'embie' in a Petri dish or frozen for a future transfer in a canister of liquid nitrogen – can be as powerful as one with a baby developing in a womb. If a pregnancy isn't created, this can feel like the loss of a baby-to-be, with all the attendant dreams, plans and hopes for its future.

'I'm so sorry. It's such a huge loss.'

'But people don't quite get that, do they?'

Helen spoke with an edge of anger I hadn't heard before.

'We did get sympathy from friends, but it was very short-lived. I didn't tell my parents as I couldn't bear to break Dad's heart, and he wasn't feeling well at the time. Most people just focused on the fact we could crack on with the next round. And I know it's not rational, but I felt like I had failed again.'

Nick shook his head, hating to hear Helen's ready return to self-blame.

'We did the next round soon after, and that time we collected six eggs but only two good embryos were made. One was transferred and the other was good enough to freeze – thank goodness. We did get pregnant though.'

Helen reached for a couple of tissues as she began to cry silently, but she was determined to tell this part of their story despite her reliving what I already knew to be a miscarriage.

'We had a scan at seven weeks, and all was well. The heartbeat was strong, the size just right. We told a few people, including Mum and Dad this time, and even began to start making very tentative plans – whether to book a holiday later in the year. I felt dreadful as well, really sick and utterly exhausted. The clinic discharged us and we were passed on to the hospital to be a "normal" pregnant couple. But when we went for our twelve-week scan, there was no heartbeat.'

'Missed miscarriages' like this are a particularly cruel version of any unwanted pregnancy loss. There's often no warning before a parent-to-be finds out, and many may have spent two long months excited to see their tiny baby wriggling on an ultrasound screen. Leaving the twelve-week scan with a grainy black-and-white image of a two-inch human also marks the transition to the second trimester, where there is a significantly lower risk of miscarriage.

'It was such a shock. I was feeling every symptom in the book, and we were so confident after the first scan.'

'I'm so sorry. You can't forget an event like that.'

Helen blew her nose and nodded.

'No, you can't. I won't ever forget how the sonographer was too quiet for my liking, and that she wouldn't answer my questions. She didn't even look at us when she told us the news. She just said, "I can't find a heartbeat. It looks like the embryo ceased to develop after nine weeks." She then left the room to get someone else while I lay there, completely shocked and barely covered from the waist down. I didn't know whether to get dressed or not.'

Nick took over.

'I didn't know what to do either. I just stood there feeling useless. And like I'd been punched in the stomach. I don't think English was her first language, but her words were pretty brutal. That was our baby who died. Not an embryo ceasing anything.'

Saddened to hear yet another diagnosis of a missed miscarriage being badly handled, I stated the obvious.

'Those were inadequate words. I'm so sorry.'

'We went into that room nervous, but also full of hope. We left completely hollowed out. I tried so hard to keep it together for Hels, but I couldn't take it all in. I then had to un-tell everyone, before all the enquiries about the scan started coming in. So many people were rooting for us by then. It's so silly, but we felt like we'd let people down again.'

Helen cleared her throat and was ready to speak.

'I hated telling my parents the most as Dad was having a check-up that week. I knew he'd be upset, but also that he'd want to protect me from that. He'd be the last person on earth to say I'd let him down, but I can't forgive myself for what I put him through. I was a difficult teen and I used to row with Mum a lot. I cringe when I think of the things I did – I'd run out of the house without telling them where I was going and disappear for days, and I even nicked money from my mum's purse a few times. I was dreadful!'

'Maybe your problematic behaviour was your solution to something. What was going on at the time?'

'I got caught up in the wrong crowd for a bit and my first boyfriend was really bad news. He treated me terribly and turned me against my family. We can laugh about it now, but I still hate myself for it. Dad was always the peacemaker at home and never, ever shouted at me once. I know I really put him through the wringer. I can't help thinking that the stress I caused weakened him and made him more susceptible to cancer.'

We often turn to such irrational thinking when we are trying to make sense of traumatic truths. Joan Didion writes of this in her extraordinary memoir *The Year of Magical Thinking* as she looks back on the time immediately following her husband's death: 'I was thinking as small children think, as if my thoughts or wishes had the power to reverse the narrative, change the outcome.' She explores the human capacity to criticise ourselves for not doing enough to prevent the death of our loved ones and it didn't surprise me to hear this line of Helen's thinking.

They told me how the miscarriage took an enormous toll on them both: Nick's mood plummeted and Helen became increasingly anxious. At first she worried excessively about her future fertility, and the chances of another pregnancy, but her anxiety – as anxiety tends to do – seeped through to other areas of her life: she avoided speaking with friends for fear of being boring, or, even worse, being pitied.

While some miscarriages happen suddenly and quickly, and sometimes even painlessly, missed miscarriages need medical management, and Helen and Nick had to decide how Helen's body would let go of their baby in the midst of their emotional turmoil. Some couples trust nature to take its course, while others take medication or elect to have surgery.

'We were told our options and given a leaflet. I couldn't bear the idea of walking around for days still sort of pregnant, so I went for the medication option. The leaflet referred to my "products of conception" being dealt with in different ways. I felt sick reading that. It seemed to confirm that my pregnancy wasn't good enough. It was as if I couldn't even make a baby.'

Helen looked at Nick, who took over.

'I took the leaflet off Helen and tore it up.'

Along with the language of failure, another abiding medical phrase that creates so much unnecessary distress is 'products of conception'. When a doctor used that phrase with me, I genuinely worried my womb had produced inanimate objects. Out-of-date leaflets and jarring words spoken by medics who don't know better can, and do, wound. The confused couple then went home, prescribed pills in hand, and went through the painful and lengthy process of bleeding and cramping to give birth to their baby.

'I still can't believe how much it hurt. The painkillers didn't touch the sides and I was left wondering if I was being a lightweight. And then I became obsessed with the idea that I shouldn't have carried on swimming, that the chemicals in the pool had somehow caused the miscarriage. Or that I should have taken days off sick when I felt truly awful.'

It didn't take Helen long, when she told this story, to reprimand herself, nor is she alone in doing so. In 2015, the baby-loss charity Tommy's published the results of their #MisCOURAGE campaign exploring the experience of miscarriage and 79 per cent of the six thousand participants described feeling like they had failed. The academic and critic Emilie Pine writes of her infertility and miscarriage in 'From the Baby Years' in her stunning essay collection *Notes to Self.* She describes her difficult decision to stop trying to conceive, and although she feels liberated by this choice, it is freighted with a similar sense of non-success: 'But the truth, what I have accepted, is this: I can try to have a baby and I can fail every month and be unhappy. Or I can try not-try to have a baby and not-fail every month.'

Nick also felt his own version of this.

'It was awful to see Helen in so much pain, and I've never seen so much blood in my life. I felt useless, yet again. I couldn't do anything but rub her back and wish it was all over.'

I know there is no solution to the grief of losing a baby, whether that is a baby in mind that is yearned for, or one already developing in a woman's body. But I do know that couples would not turn against themselves so critically, and readily, if infertility and pregnancy loss were treated as a normal – and desperately sad – trajectory of our reproductive lives.

Although I'd heard about the couple's joint desire to become parents, I also wanted to hear how they described it individually, so that I could understand the complexity for each of them.

Many of us imagine becoming parents from a tender age. Helen could reflect on this easily.

'I remember always wanting to be a mum. I was two when my sister arrived and Mum expected me to resent her, but I didn't. I just wanted to cuddle her and feed her all the time. Apparently, I was always "playing Mummy". And then I started babysitting my neighbour's kids when I was about twelve. I loved looking after them and I remember pretending they were mine! When I got back on the rails after my crazy years, I did lots of childcare and always knew I wanted to be an early years teacher.'

'And what about you, Nick? Did you imagine being a father when you were a boy?'

This isn't a question usually asked of men, and we don't expect them to experience broodiness. Instead, we assume them to be virile and fertile, and then bystanders to their female partners' wishes before and during pregnancy, and even after birth. A maternal man is judged as heroic or even adorable, and a gay man similarly lionised or instead judged dimly for wanting to parent outside of the heteronormative dictates of our culture.

'I did grow up assuming I'd be a dad, but I think that came from Mum. I'm an only child, and it's only recently, since we've been through everything, that she has opened up and told me that she and Dad tried for more children. I think it was a huge loss to her and she worked hard to cover it up. She often told me that I was deliberately an "only". I never quite believed it though; it didn't ring true.'

In my experience, the cultural silencing of infertility and pregnancy loss stories means that they are often told for the first time only when another person shares their own. When Nick was growing up, there was a far harsher social expectation to be silent about such pain. I guessed that his mother felt emboldened to speak up by Nick's candour: infertility stories beget infertility stories.

'When she told me, things made more sense. I remember finding a suitcase of my baby clothes in my mum's wardrobe when I was playing hide-and-seek with my cousin. When Mum found us looking through it, she told me that she had kept them for both of us, for when we'd have our own children. I wasn't convinced, though, as she was teary as she said it.'

These days, parents are rightly encouraged to be open with their children about siblings who didn't make it into the world. We have an uncanny ability to pick up on our parents' unexpressed feelings – including the grief of infertility and pregnancy loss – and we can feel responsible for them, without ever fully understanding why. In Nick's case, he clearly understood how precious he was, but I wondered if this made him particularly keen to repair the loss of his siblings for his mum, by producing grandchildren.

'She'd often say, "When you are a dad . . . " or "When I'm a grandma . . . " So I guess I grew up thinking it was something I was destined to do.'

Nick then took Helen's hand again, as a means to steady a feeling that I could see he was literally swallowing down.

'And this is another thing I berate myself about. Helen's never wobbled about us having a baby but I've wanted to throw in the towel more than once. And I know it sounds silly, but I worry that my doubts have had an effect on us – as if somehow the universe knows about my uncertainty and so is holding back on giving us a baby.'

Just as Helen's mind had succumbed to magical thinking in relation to the cause of her father's illness and her miscarriage, Nick's thinking also turned magical as a means to cope with the unknown reasons for their loss.

'There's no known reason for your losses, and there's not much that you can do to guarantee a live birth. It's natural for you to grab something that feels like it's concrete and – falsely – within your control, like your lack of conviction.'

I regularly have conversations about the desire – or not – to have a child, but most often with women. It's not always as straightforward as a mild or an all-consuming hunger to be pregnant. I've also heard many other reasons: a determination to parent differently from what we experienced ourselves; wanting to leave a meaningful legacy after death; cementing love for a partner or pleasing him or her; and in the case of one client I had, in order to have company in a painfully lonely life.

The desire to procreate has an inescapable cultural component as well. Our supposedly liberal Western values aren't immune to the antiquated pressure to bear fruit, despite claims of more enlightened views: women are judged dimly if they don't become mothers. The feminist and author Adrienne Rich wrote in the *New York Times* back in 1976 that 'the "non-mothering" woman is seen as deviant' and I don't think that view has changed much since then.

Men who don't become fathers are judged in a different, but similarly pejorative, way. Mainstream religions endorse pronatalism on their own spiritual grounds, and some national governments encourage childbearing with economic leverage or plainly moralistic appeals. Even my own profession, in certain theoretical circles, is guilty of pathologising a woman's choice not to be a mother, and even her inability to birth live babies.

Nick continued, a little steadier in voice. 'I think Mum felt that she had really let me down for being an "only". And I know now it had a big effect on her self-esteem. She thinks badly of herself all the time. She told me that her sister had once said to her, "One child doesn't make a family, but two or more children will." I don't think she meant it to be cruel and was just encouraging my mum to keep trying.'

While Helen and Nick really needed to talk through the private hell they had gone through over the previous few years, they had also come to see me with a view to gathering strength for their next attempt at a pregnancy. They had one frozen embryo to transfer, and now had to pay privately to arrange this. Although far cheaper than a full IVF cycle, paying for the transfer took them to the limit of their savings. Facing the prospect of their last assisted conception for a while, the couple understandably felt that the stakes were high.

For a few weeks we talked about ways to manage the

inevitable anxieties of another potential pregnancy, alongside conversations that helped to process their ongoing grief for their losses. Helen began to prepare her body as best she could but she felt conflicted by the pressure she felt to improve her chances of a live birth – which was largely created by products and treatments promoted online.

Many of these add-ons to fertility treatment are anecdotally beneficial rather than data-driven but are understandably seductive to desperately vulnerable people. The Human Fertilisation and Embryology Authority have recently instituted a traffic-light system to signal their level of endorsement (with a red warning against those with no robust evidence). But couples longing to be pregnant can still berate themselves if they don't try everything.

'I've read about these herbs some women take, and about immunology testing. There's even a woman who charges a fortune to do hands-on healing of wombs. We can't afford anything extra but I worry that I'm not trying hard enough, or that I'll regret not trying to maximise my chances.'

When I talk to couples trying to conceive naturally, I'm generally not privy to the details of their sex life. We may talk about the fact that sex can become passionless or perfunctory when it aims to achieve conception, but this tends to be accepted as a temporary phase. Couples undergoing fertility treatment don't have the luxury of privacy, or mystery, when it comes to the making of their babies. The breaking down of conception into distinct steps, taken over days or weeks, is obviously the topic of conversation in the fertility clinic, but can become a hot one outside it too.

Helen and Nick found it difficult to navigate the boundaries around their privacy with those who they had told about their fertility treatment. While they didn't want to be secretive about their struggles or what's involved with IVF, their candour sometimes came at the cost of having to deal with unsolicited advice. In one session, shortly before their transfer, Helen voiced a pile-up of frustrations with unusual force.

'If one more person tells me that I should "just relax this time" and it will happen ... Or if I'm told about another "amazing supplement" or meditation practice that I *have* to use because it got someone's friend pregnant ... I know people mean well, but Nick doesn't get told to relax or meditate! I just feel like I'm doing things wrong again.'

We had talked about the unequal distribution of care, compassion and respect between men and women enough for me to know I didn't need to add anything to this. Helen went on, still fuelled with resentment.

'But the other thing that pisses me off is that it's as if our miscarriage didn't happen. I've been told more than once "At least you know you can get pregnant," and a colleague suggested that my body had now "warmed up" for this pregnancy.'

Helen looked at Nick, then back to me, saying for them both, 'Our due date is next week. We're dreading it.'

Due dates for miscarried babies are often painful days and are barely recognised or even known by others. We spoke of taking some time to mark the occasion, or even creating a ritual of remembrance, and it was then that I found out that they had named their lost baby Dora. But in her telling, Helen was soon berating herself again – her frequent self-criticism even targeted her mourning.

'I feel guilty that I'm not giving Dora the justice she deserves because I'm so caught up with getting pregnant again.'

We had a session a few days before their embryo was transferred, having done our best to prepare for the inevitable anxieties of the wait until Helen's pregnancy test. This wasn't an unfamiliar interval of time for the couple to endure, but unlike scores of previous waiting periods it was charged with a different type of frenzied hope. We agreed to meet a month later because, as Nick suggested, 'either way, we'll need to think things through again'.

I tend to keep communication with my clients to a minimum between sessions, as a part of my effort to maintain the boundaries of the therapeutic relationship. But exceptions to all my rules can and do take place, and I was delighted that Helen texted me with the good news. Or, as she put it, 'good news for now': she had a positive pregnancy test.

When I next opened the door to them, I couldn't help but be aware that all might not be well – a miscarriage can happen even hours after a positive pregnancy test and, just like Helen and Nick, I couldn't wholeheartedly believe that their test result would lead to a live birth. My work, and own experiences, have diminished my optimism. But another way of looking at it is that I'm realistic: infertility and pregnancy losses are an integral part of our reproductive lives and one in four pregnancies do end before twenty-four weeks.

Every couple I talk to experiences some level of anxiety during pregnancies after previous loss. The first twelve weeks are particularly fraught, when the risk of miscarriage is at its highest and pregnancy symptoms can slow the experience of time down to an excruciating near halt. Helen and Nick felt understandably ambivalent about bonding with their unborn baby in case another heartbreak was waiting in the wings.

But the twelve-week scan went well, and both built up a little more faith in becoming parents. Their increasing resilience meant that we then agreed to meet a few times more during the remainder of the pregnancy.

By twenty-four weeks of pregnancy, Helen's bump became obvious to my eye. As tempted as I was to celebrate the growth of her baby, I held back from doing so until I could gauge how she felt about her changing body being noticed. Some women want to share their maternal body with the world, but others can feel more protective and cautious – especially after pregnancy loss.

Also, I didn't want to heighten the sense of surveillance that our culture encourages towards pregnant bodies. Élisabeth Badinter writes in her wonderful polemic about the pressures upon modern motherhood, *The Conflict*: 'Like a postulant taking the veil, the future mother no longer belongs to herself. Her worldly life has come to an end, something only God and a baby have the power to achieve.' Alongside the 'no longer belonging to herself' comes a strong sense of self-reproach for a pregnant woman if anything harms her pregnancy – even if this harm couldn't definitively be traced back to her as a cause. I made the right call by saying nothing, as Helen brought the issue up herself, while stroking her newly rounded belly.

'We were at a friend's birthday party at the weekend, and I treated myself to a small glass of Prosecco. I had barely put it to my lips when a woman next to me raised her eyebrows, cocked her head to the side and asked if I was drinking alcohol. I was furious, but then quickly felt really guilty and ended up giving it to Nick.'

Nick squeezed Helen's spare hand, noting, 'We were just

saying on the way here how everyone has something to say now we are established in pregnancy, but so many had nothing to say when we were reeling from not being pregnant.'

I knew this phenomenon so well. Helen's pregnancy ushered in, at long last, a cultural success, but the nagging feeling of their failures at previous conceptions and pregnancy were hovering near by, ready to latch on to other self-diagnosed wrongs.

It is one of the immense privileges of my job to be so intimately involved with the emotional efforts to conceive a longed-for baby, and then to be privy to a growth chart or scan picture, and descriptions of limb movements and attributions of a developing baby's character. Helen and Nick knew their baby was a boy, and I felt his growing presence in the room with us during the few more times that we met. I was excited for the couple to end our therapy, but our imminent goodbye saddened me too, as I had become very fond of them. However, when I opened the door for our final session, my heart hit the ground: Helen looked pale and the darkness under her eyes suggested something dreadful had happened.

As the couple made their way to my consulting room, every part of me willed their baby boy to be safe and well. Yet I also knew it was a binary outcome: if the baby was okay, something else wasn't. Helen perched at the edge of her usual seat, unable to settle further back.

'Dad's cancer's returned with a vengeance. His latest scan wasn't good at all – it's spread everywhere. They can only give him palliative care now. He's got weeks, rather than months. We knew this was coming, of course, but it doesn't make it any easier. He's promised me he's going to meet his grandson, though, and Mum's bought their train tickets to come and stay with us. They're coming a week before the due date.'

My relief that their baby was still thriving sat uneasily beside my desolation for Helen and her family. I thought of the inevitable, unbearable weight of grief that was coming her way and was unsurprised by the vein of guilt and self-condemnation that ran through her narrative as she spoke again: for being a tricky teenager, for moving away from home in Wales to London, for not being present enough during his cancer treatment.

Nick interrupted to derail her next self-attack. 'We're soon giving him the grandson he so desperately wanted to meet.'

We closed our session, and our time together, knowing that it was highly likely that I would see Helen on her own again as she mothered her newborn while losing a father. We spoke of my helping her further with the dismantling of her sense of failure as she navigated both new realms. I hoped she could restore her confidence in her body and her self, and that this compassion could flow back to her teenage self too.

A month later, Nick texted me a photo of Helen resting her head on the shoulder of an older man as they sat beside each other on a sofa. Both faces were turned towards a swaddled baby in his arms, and it was easy to see the edges of two beaming smiles.

'Hi Julia, this is Dylan, named after Helen's dad. Mother, baby and grandad doing really well. And I'm pretty chuffed too!'

Chapter Seven

Goodliness

'But do you know how old I will be by the time
I learn to really play the piano/act/paint/write a
decent play?'

Yes ... the same age you will be if you don't.

JULIA CAMERON,
The Artist's Way

When Susan first settled into her chair in my consulting room, I imagined her giving me a warm hug. It certainly wasn't something I intended to happen. Like most therapists I know, I tend to choose the giving and receiving of hugs – and touches generally – carefully. If a hug takes place at all, it is usually at the end of therapy, as a natural, and agreed, means to cement a fond farewell.

After getting to know Susan, I realised that my unusual fantasy was an unconscious response to her boundless compassion for others, and her instinct to give everyone a hug, both literally and metaphorically. But I also quickly learnt how difficult it was for her to allow any of this easy flow of compassion to be directed back to herself; she couldn't bear thinking of herself in such lovable terms. I have never believed in the adage that you can't love others unless you love yourself. Susan was proof of the opposite.

Susan came to see me on the recommendation of Elizabeth, an ex-client of mine and friend of hers, as she wanted my help with the writer's block that had been plaguing her for a few months. I've talked to many authors, scriptwriters and academics over the years, all battling with themselves in their efforts to fill the page. Ted Hughes wrote, 'The progress of any writer is marked by those moments when he manages to outwit his own inner police system which tells him what is permissible, what is possible, what is "him".' Susan wasn't aware of being bothered by any such inner police system before she came to see me, though, and was baffled by her problem that she wanted to fix.

She was quick to tell me that she did not describe herself as a writer, but she was soon to turn sixty and had hoped to fulfil a lifelong dream to write a novel by the time her birthday came around. While that was no longer possible, she at least wanted to get going as she had been plotting it in her head for years – though she was too embarrassed to tell me what it was about. I was surprised by her age, as I had guessed her to be nearer my own, more than a decade younger. She was beautiful without the embellishments of make-up, jewellery or colourful clothes that many of us rely upon to fight ageing.

Susan didn't seem to care about publishing her writing, or who would ultimately read it, but was far more bothered by the fact that she was unable to translate her ideas onto paper.

Clearly a competent and upbeat woman, being stymied was unusual for her and was getting her down.

'It's silly, really, you must talk to people about far more serious things. But I just don't understand why I can't get on with it. I'm so good at getting on with things usually! And then I hate feeling down about it, it is so selfish. There are many more important things to worry about than my stupid dream to write.'

'Selfish?'

'Well, I mean really, it is. I'm embarrassed to be sitting here. Stories pour out of my head usually. I always had plenty to tell my children and now I do with my grandchildren. And for the first time in forty years I actually have time to put one down on paper, but each time I try, I face the tyranny of the blank page.'

'Tyranny is a strong word to use.'

'Oh, slip of the tongue! I should be more careful with my words when talking to a therapist. It's not like me to be stuck with anything, nor like me to be so upset about something that really doesn't matter. I'm just confused, and Elizabeth thought you could help me puzzle it out.'

I was struck by how dismissive Susan was about a lifelong dream, and also by her ready self-deprecation towards being concerned about it. I could immediately sense how easy it was for her to criticise herself for spending too much time on herself, and guessed that even looking in the mirror felt indulgent.

'Not like you to get upset?'

'I'm generally a very happy person. I've never felt so distracted and upset as I have of late. It was a bit tough for a couple of years before my menopause, but that was because of that, so it all made sense and I just got on with it.'

'I imagine you have thought about the possible reasons as to why you can't write. There's nothing else going on right now that could explain it?'

Susan looked flummoxed, widening her eyes and broadening her ready smile.

'I've got nothing to complain about. I'm so blessed. I've got a great marriage, a loving family. We don't have to worry about money, or our health. I'm fit as a fiddle. But I heard an author on the radio talk about how his therapy helped him when he was blocked. So I asked Elizabeth if she thought it might help me.'

'Sounds like she did think so.'

'She's always nagging me to talk about myself, so I guess I knew what her answer was going to be. I'm no use to anybody being forlorn, and I have to sort myself out soon. If I'm not going to write anything after all, I'll have to think of something else more useful to do.'

Some authors I have worked with have been frustrated or even angry about their creative mind letting them down, whereas others have felt defeated by not knowing how to approach their material. Many I meet feel very stressed, or anxious, especially if there's a professional obligation to produce work for a deadline. Susan could only describe a genuine confusion at her inability to translate her ideas onto the page, and she framed this as a potential nuisance to others, including me.

'Why do you have more time now?'

'The youngest of my babies has left home! Rob has gone to university. I know I'm naughty because I did lots for him right until he left – cooking and cleaning and driving him around – but it was my last chance and I savoured it. So my nest is empty after nearly forty years.'

A flash of sadness punctuated Susan's speech.

'How full was your nest?'

'We've got five kids. I had my oldest two – twins – when I was twenty-one, the next two in my mid-twenties, and then Rob snuck in when I wasn't looking when I was forty-one. I've got five grandchildren – they come and stay quite often, but it's not the same, of course.'

'It sounds like you have had, and still have, a lot of people who you think about and care about. It makes me wonder if you have had enough of a chance to think and care about yourself over the years.'

Ignoring my tentative question, Susan ploughed on.

'I have loved every moment of being a mum and I love being a grandmother. It's what I was destined to do. But when it comes to writing, I worry that I've strayed into an area that I shouldn't have. But what else? I should achieve something with the next chunk of my life while I'm still fit and strong. Women these days are becoming mothers for the first time at fifty and retiring later than ever before. I have to come up with something.'

Therapists tend to pounce on words like should, ought and must as clues to the existence of our clients' internal critics. At first, many people tell me that these words come from themselves, but on further investigation they can nearly always be traced back to messaging from somewhere outside themselves: other people or the wider culture. I agreed with Susan's description of a contemporary pressure on women to postpone old age as best they can, but I focused on her first statement as it seemed to be more personal.

'Who says you have strayed into an area that you shouldn't?'

Susan shrugged her shoulders and laughed. 'I don't know. But do you think he or she has anything to do with my writer's block?'

I did think so, but without knowing more about him or her or any of the other influences in the mix, I couldn't commit to a confident hypothesis yet.

'Perhaps. But we'll have a better idea after talking more, and after finding out what you may not realise you bring to the blank page.'

Given that Susan had made it very clear that she didn't like to spend too much time thinking about herself in any depth, I figured that she might struggle with this plan.

I always looked forward to my sessions with Susan. There's an idea among therapists that clients turn up in our consulting rooms at the right time in order to teach us what it is we need to pay attention to in our own lives. In Susan's case, it was her can-do attitude that I needed when we first met. I was being unusually negative and pessimistic about committing to a few projects. I took a conscious note of my admiration for – and sometimes envy of – her outlook on life, while knowing from experience that it could also be a possible means to avoid turning inwards.

She swam every morning before the house stirred, and she had taught swimming to adults with learning disabilities one evening a week for many years. She regularly helped look after her grandchildren as well as managing the payroll of her husband's business and bearing the lion's share of domestic tasks. One week she shared with me her delight at having taken in a student lodger with a view to helping him improve his English. She batted away my remark that she was feathering her nest again.

Susan had clearly spent her adult life caring for others, and I wanted to know more about this so that I could get a better idea of whether her writer's block was related to the recent change of gear that her son's departure had prompted.

'Graham and I have known each other most of our lives – we were literally childhood sweethearts. He lived at the end of my road and we started walking to school together when we were at primary school. I still remember the day he first waited for me at the corner. And then our brothers and sisters came along, and they joined us on the walk too, the line getting longer each year. We would wait for each other at the end of the day to walk back again.'

'You must be the youngest pair of sweethearts I've heard of.'

Susan laughed. 'But we weren't sweethearts for years! My parents would never have allowed that – they were *very* religious. They forbade us from being alone together, even when we were in the sixth form. We'd only walk side by side once we were out of sight of my mother's beady eyes.'

'It sounds like your parents were very strict.'

'They were. If Graham came by the house to see me, it would have to be related to homework or school, and my mother would always be standing at the door behind me, so we couldn't talk privately. We'd write notes, though, and pass them to each other at school, or on the walk to school. I used to bribe my brothers and sisters with sweets to keep them quiet if they spotted us passing notes or whispering together.'

'So how did you get together, then?'

'As soon as I left school, I got a job in a nursery. I had wanted to read English at university but that was out of the question. I was good at English and had my head in a book whenever I could, but my parents would never have let me do something so wild and indulgent. However, working meant I got a bit more independence, and I could see more of Graham. We were together for a couple of years after we left school before we told my parents.'

'How did that go?'

'It meant getting married very quickly. They wouldn't let me out of their sight otherwise. But they liked Graham, mainly because he came from a good Christian family, and he also knew how to keep them on side, though as soon as we could, we moved out of the area – I was desperate to get away, as you can imagine. I got a job at another nursery and Graham joined an estate agency. The rest, as they say, is history.'

As she reflected on the beginning of her adult life, it seemed as if Susan was piecing it together for the first time. She clearly wasn't used to talking through her story.

'I got pregnant on our honeymoon: I barely knew it was possible; we were so naïve. I was only twenty, just a bit older than Rob is. It seems extraordinary to think of it now. And then it turned out to be twins – Anna and Vicky – so we were in quite deep from the start. Anna was tiny and needed to stay in hospital for a few weeks. And then she needed quite a bit of help feeding and settling.'

'What a worry. And with Vicky to look after as well.'

'I still vividly remember that first year, pacing our bedroom holding a crying Anna on one shoulder, with Vicky under the other arm as she fed. Graham was determined to set up his own estate agency, so he was working flat out trying to prove himself and learn as much as he could. He has always wanted to put lots of bread on our table.'

'We can often underestimate how tough it is on a mum to have a baby who needs a lot of attention. That must have been a stressful time,' I said.

My kindly observation slid off Susan.

'Well, I guess it was more of the same really. I had had a good run of looking after babies at home when I was growing up. I was the oldest of five and often helped look after my sisters and brothers. Sometimes there were other babies and children to look after too, as we often had other families staying with us.'

'It sounds like you were introduced to caring for others early on.'

'I suppose so, yes. My parents were always busy, so we all had to step up from an early age. I could change a nappy with my eyes closed by the time I was seven or eight. My youngest brother was only ten when I left home. When the twins arrived, in some ways it was water off a duck's back. I was used to babies and broken nights.'

'When it was your turn, did you have any help from the family members who you had helped so much?'

I suspected the answer to this was no, as there was a sense of sadness around Susan's parents when she referred to them, but I wanted to test what the temperature was like between them after she had left home. Again, Susan laughed.

'Not really, no. But that was okay. I wasn't in a position to ask anyway. Graham and I chose a different path from them, and also from the one they had hoped I would pursue. When I moved away, my parents were really disappointed. They were good people, and they loved me, but their beliefs got in the way of us being close. It's sad how things turned out, but there you go. They died within months of each other a few years back.'

We had much more to talk about when it came to her parents. There were plenty of clues that hinted at a family culture of censorship and judgement, and I wanted to know how this was connected to Susan's discomfort at examining her inner world. She presented a double whammy I commonly come up against: a criticism of oneself for being in the consulting room in the first place. It would take more time before she would realise that she was actually criticising herself for criticising herself.

Susan seemed to be an endless source of service to others, although she didn't describe her role in these terms. Her weekly updates were made up of stories of her running errands or doing favours for her family, friends, neighbours and new lodger. She would shy away from my attempts to focus her thoughts and feelings on herself by asking questions about *my* own health and wellbeing. I was sneezing with mild hay fever one week and she arrived at our next session with a small tub of beeswax ointment for me.

This wasn't the first gift. She often arrived with 'a little something' from her garden or her kitchen – herbs, plants or a pot of home-made pickle. Gifts from the client to the therapist are a source of discussion and debate with our supervisors and colleagues when we share clinical work anonymously: what they symbolise, how they reflect upon the relationship between a therapist and client, and also whether it's appropriate to accept them or not. Therapists can mine potential meaning from all iterations of interactions – such as leaving something behind in a consulting room in an unconscious bid to be remembered.

I was sure that Susan was genuinely caring and compassionate. I never felt that she was trying to prove anything to me or conveying any trace of martyrdom when she told me of the time and effort that her kindnesses took. When she gave me a gift, it always felt like genuine thoughtfulness. But while her boundless giving didn't feel contrived, I had a hunch that alongside her natural instincts there was also a fear of *not* being generous, as if she was acting on a strict moral order that forbade giving to herself.

After handing me the ointment, Susan explained how to use it. 'Take a tiny amount and rub it around the edge of your nostrils: that's how it traps the pollen. It's made from ... Oh, sorry, I'll stop there. It's all in the leaflet and I'm sure you can read it. It's just the teacher in me coming out.'

'Ah, the nursery and swimming teacher?'

She quietly tutted, as if to tell herself off, and then laughed as she often did.

'Yes, there's that. But I also home-schooled four of my kids. I can still slip into teacher mode at times – forgive me.'

In my mind, this was no small detail, and I was curious as to why she hadn't told me this when we had talked extensively about her busy family life. As usual, she brushed it off as nothing special.

'That's not for the faint-hearted. Why did you do home school?'

'Anna had been through so much as a baby with her feeding issues and it turned out she had a problem with her stomach. When she was three, she had an operation and I think the whole experience of being in hospital, and of being in so much discomfort, really knocked her confidence. She hated being separated from me after that.'

'I'm sorry to hear that. That must have been worrying for you.'

It didn't surprise me that my comment about Susan's emotional welfare was immediately redirected to someone else.

'Poor Anna: little thing was so poorly, and then so scared about the world. She couldn't settle at school when she started, and after a term of her being so unhappy we decided to pull her out. Vicky refused to be separated from her; they were so close that they even spoke their own language. I had just had Pippa then too, so it suited me to have them both at home rather than doing the school run as well. And six months after Pippa was born, I was pregnant again with Harry.'

Susan paused, again seemingly thinking back on these years afresh.

'Actually, that was a very busy time because Graham's business took a real tumble. I was trying to help him out as well. I took his clients to view properties at the weekend, usually with one of the babies in a sling, and I did a bit of budgeting and marketing for him.'

'I'm amazed by how much you juggled.'

As usual, Susan seemed resistant to adjusting her focus towards herself. She often looked puzzled by my observations about her remarkable output, and I had to take care that these comments weren't tangled up with my occasional private guilt about my different style of mothering. After each of my sons was born, I returned to work within weeks, and I know I would never have considered home schooling for fear of compromising my personal and professional ambitions.

'I ended up schooling them right through – the only decent secondary school near us was a church school, and there was no way on earth I was sending my children there. By the time it was Rob's turn, there was a new school which had opened and he really wanted to go. I did feel guilty letting him go, though, as he didn't get all that time with me the others got.'

Susan usually spoke with such warmth, but her voice changed register when she talked about the church school.

'What was wrong with the church school?'

'Oh, nothing per se. Long story, really. It's just fair to say that the church and I don't see eye to eye any more. I had more than my fair share of religion growing up, so I was determined to make sure that my kids felt free to choose what they wanted to believe in, rather than have others do that for them. I wanted them to have the opposite of what I had.'

Susan seemed breezy as she said this, but it sounded as if her religious upbringing had not actually been a breeze. In telling me that she had had little choice in what she could believe in growing up, she was perhaps suggesting that a police system existed in her. I wasn't surprised to hear of a long story she hadn't yet told, as clients can take time to share their experiences with me – especially those who are unused to sharing them.

Susan continued to stall when it came to her writing. I love the work of Gillie Bolton, who teaches and practises writing for therapeutic benefit. We looked together at some of her prompts to tackle blocks head-on and Susan dutifully noted some exercises down, but just as insomnia can ruin the once pleasant sight of an inviting bed, even catching a glimpse of her laptop would make Susan fret. She avoided the blank page by helping others, and if Graham didn't need her for his business, a daughter, son, friend, grandchild or neighbour would call on her instead.

Susan's looming sixtieth birthday party gave her even more

reasons to avoid thinking about her writing and herself. I tried hard to discover how she wanted to celebrate this milestone, but she was more preoccupied with throwing a party to please her friends and family, rather than herself. Even my attempts to find out what she wanted to wear were batted away in favour of talking through the adjustments she was making to Anna's vintage dress and her grandchildren's childcare on the night. While I knew she would dislike drawing too much attention to herself, she also seemed to think her age cast her aside.

'I'm sixty, for goodness' sake. I really can't pretend to be as attractive as my daughters.'

I encouraged her to think about saying no or not now to others who relied on her, without feeling guilty or selfish. But she also seemed to assume that I would come down heavily on her for not trying hard enough to find time to write. When she described to me how busy her week had been, it sounded like an earnest apology for letting me down.

'You really don't have to build a case for the defence here. I'm not going to think badly of you for not writing anything,' I said in one session.

Susan laughed at herself in a way I had got to know so well. 'Some old habits die hard.'

'Perhaps you imagine me to be your strict mother? Or father?'

Susan hadn't been willing to offer up much information about her parents in previous conversations. But this time, weeks into our meetings, she was more ready to look at what they had represented to her.

'Maybe you are right – I do hate to let people down. My parents were emphatic about words being bonds.'

Susan paused as she reminded herself of this powerful edict.

'They *were* really good people, but they were deeply religious and Godfearing, you see. We all had to live by many rules: what to wear, what to eat, when to sleep, even what to think. And, of course, what to pray about and when – there was a timetable for that. God ruled every moment of their lives, and that meant our lives too.'

Susan shuddered a little, as if freeing herself from shackles.

'Can you tell me more what that was like for you growing up under God's rule?'

'For as long as I can remember I was told there was only one way to get to heaven, and if we didn't follow it we'd be doomed. I was a very serious little girl and I believed what I was told. We went to a local Church of England school that was more liberal than our own small church, though, and I would pray for my classmates who didn't take God as seriously as me. I worried about them terribly.'

'What a heavy burden for a child.'

'It was awful. I remember thinking they would go to hell if they didn't see the light, like me. I thought that I was normal and the others weren't. I couldn't celebrate my birthday, or have friends over to play, or toys, or a skipping rope. I didn't even know what fizzy drinks or dark chocolate were like until I was married! I couldn't cook anything apart from the simplest things.'

It's not unusual to wait for a full picture of a childhood to emerge. Sometimes it can take months or years before clients fill in gaps with details, depending on their comfort – conscious or unconscious – with revisiting their past. While Susan's reticence about her own past may have had a lot to do with her ready criticism of herself for being self-indulgent, it was also bound up with the discomfort her memories brought.

In her memoir *Educated*, Tara Westover writes of her own experiences of being brought up in a fundamentalist household: 'My life was narrated for me by others. Their voices were forceful, emphatic, absolute. It had never occurred to me that my voice might be as strong as theirs.' Westover's pursuit of education became her salvation from the crippling strictures of her family's beliefs and Susan's determination to broaden the minds of her own children through schooling them herself reminded me of Westover's story.

'When did you begin to think differently?'

'In my early teens. Most of the kids thought I was odd, of course, and I probably seemed a bit snooty because I was judging them all the time. But a couple of girls in my class wanted to understand me, and they became my friends, showing me different ways. But it was mainly Graham who opened my mind – he was raised Christian, but a liberal and tolerant and curious one. His family allowed him to question and doubt things, and he encouraged me to do the same. God didn't rule every aspect of his life.'

'I take it you couldn't air your doubts at home?'

'Absolutely not! There was never any room for discussion, and I would have been reprimanded for challenging anyone on anything. The Bible, or one interpretation of it anyway, ruled our lives, and then, on top of that, there was what God willed or not. The Seniors had the last word on everything – they would make anything grey into black or white.'

As Susan told me more, I felt like we'd hit the rich seam she had been avoiding.

'The Seniors?'

'The men who led our church. My father became one when I was really young – he was the good cop really, as he was far kinder than the others. It was a very small church, run out of a house in town, just a few doors down from our own. We spent most of our free time there – after school, weekends and a lot of the holidays. The women and girls were mainly cooking and cleaning and looking after the little ones.'

'And the boys?'

They would be studying the Bible with the men or doing the physical work in or around the house, such as DIY or gardening. It wasn't all bad though: we had lots of fun together and we looked out for each other. I was never bored or lonely growing up.'

'It makes me wonder how natural it was to have a big family of your own.'

'Yes, I grew up believing that all the members of the church were an extended family – we'd call all the women aunts and the men uncles, and we were all brothers or sisters. Women were expected to help out with each other's children. I honestly don't remember a time when it was just the seven of us.'

'It sounds like there was nowhere to hide if you wanted to though. Could you have any privacy?' I meant physical privacy, but also privacy in her mind.

'It's funny you should say that about hiding, because one memory that sticks out from back then is when I got into serious trouble. I must have been about ten, and I wanted some peace and quiet one day to finish a book I had borrowed from the school library. I took the book and a torch and climbed into a cupboard in a room at the top of the church house. There was always a job that I should have been doing, so I must have known I was risking trouble.'

'I'm guessing you were found.'

'An auntie found me, and she was absolutely furious – she twisted my ear and dragged me to my mother. Then they both went to tell a Senior, although I remember my mother feeling bad for me. I was summoned to see some of the Seniors in their creepy meeting room, and I was lectured about how selfish I was to worry others, and sinful for not being available to be of service to others. My father wasn't there, which was a shame as he would have been a softer touch. I had extra cleaning duties for weeks, and hours of extra prayers. It's funny how well I remember it.'

Memories can be sharp if they evoke strong feelings, so I wasn't as surprised as Susan. If the feelings are too strong, however – as with trauma – memories can be shattered, obscured or buried.

'That sounds both cruel and humiliating.'

I was relieved that, this time, Susan didn't bat my words. Hearing more about her childhood brought home to me what a fantastic job she had done at distancing herself from the lack of compassion she had experienced from her own parents. Her parenting was clearly very different.

'I haven't thought about this for years. But I reckon if I hadn't gone to hide, I would have felt bad for even wanting to finish my book. The Seniors, and God, were inside my head at all times you see, watching my thoughts. It meant I was never completely free of sin.'

'How could you be? We all have mean, irrational and bizarre thoughts flying around our minds at times. They don't make us mean, irrational or bizarre though.'

'I felt guilty *all the time*. I think that's why we all kept so busy: to keep the sins at bay.'

It seemed that Susan was still, unconsciously, trying to

avoid incurring the wrath of God even though she had consciously rejected His punishing role in her life. Serving herself, by writing her novel, rather than serving others, stirred up a buried belief in her innate badness – just as reading a book had when she was ten.

Professor Paul Gilbert is a psychologist who views our mental health through the lens of evolution, and he describes how our brains have developed certain algorithms to survive and thrive. One of these is an innate response to submit to a dominant force: 'if powerful, submit'. He notes how our relationship to gods throughout history has been shaped by this particular hardwiring, and that we have consistently subordinated ourselves to the powerful forces we believe to be behind our origins.

This instinct to submit to gods means that we acknowledge and accept their superior powers, and also strive to appease them, sometimes through extraordinary means: I have shuddered at the graffiti depicting human sacrifices at the ancient Mayan site of Temple II, Tikal in the Guatemalan forest. But appeasing the gods in such dramatic, and less dramatic, ways – such as how Susan's family slavishly followed their reading of the Bible – doesn't always work. Untimely deaths and accidents, floods and fires – and global pandemics – still happen. So, Gilbert notes, in response to being let down by our efforts, we tend to turn towards scapegoats or sinners instead.

'I think that a part of you still believes it's not okay to be of service to yourself, as opposed to others,' I said. 'You won't be criticised for your writing by anyone but yourself now. I want you to recognise and accept that you are fully entitled to be included in the humanity you care for so deeply.'

Susan paused to take this in.

'That's what Elizabeth says to me. She thinks I still believe in a god I say I don't believe in.'

'I wish you could commit to spending more time thinking about that. Letting that idea infuse your thoughts and actions.'

I had real hope this would become easier for her. As with everything we fear doing, we tend to overestimate the risks of doing so, while underestimating our strengths. The imminent arrival of her birthday also allowed me to test Susan's willingness to attend to her desires more, and to reflect upon what she missed out on.

With her sixtieth party just a couple of weeks away, I asked Susan to tell me about birthdays she had as a child.

'We weren't allowed to celebrate anyone's birthday growing up, so they were just another day. In fact, it was frowned upon to even mention them. I remember dreading someone asking when mine was – I didn't want to lie, of course, because that would mean going to hell! But I didn't want to tell the truth, in case I got a card or present, and was then told off by a family member. I remember a teacher asking me once, and all I could do was stare at the ground and say nothing at all.'

Even though Susan behaved differently regarding birthdays now, she had passed our culturally accepted milestones – turning eighteen, twenty-one, thirty, forty, fifty – without any fuss. She was invariably caught up with an ongoing list of cake-making, present-wrapping and party organisation for the frequent celebrations for her children, grandchildren and Graham instead. I was pleased, but also surprised, by her willingness to celebrate herself this time.

'So how were you persuaded to mark turning sixty?'

'Graham and the kids got together and strong-armed me. I thought it was a bit odd when I came back from the super-market one Saturday and they were all there. Rob was at uni, but they got him online. Harry wouldn't say boo to a goose usually, but he read me the riot act. He said how important it was for *them* to celebrate and have an excuse to get together. Put like that, I had to give in, but I made them promise that I wouldn't have to make a speech or be the centre of attention. And also that I could help out. I know how much work goes into parties!'

We talked through many of Susan's worries about the catering and the music, the invitations and the complicated travel plans for some of her guests. More than once I had to remind myself – and her – that it was a party meant *for her*, and that she was entitled to choose her favourite food, the people to invite and a playlist to her own liking. Thinking about her own needs had been anathema to her, but she was warming to the idea slowly. She also began sharing her feel-ings about ageing.

'It's all right for Graham – he's become a silver fox without trying. But I've never been comfortable making the effort women seem to have to make. I guess it goes back to never being allowed to look in the mirror growing up. But I look at my friends around my age, whitening their teeth and injecting Botox into their faces. I don't want to do any of that, but I risk becoming invisible if I don't.'

As I listened, my mind went to the anti-ageing eye cream I rub in each morning, and the expensive efforts to disguise my grey hairs among sunny blond highlights. My vanity feels to be of my own making, but it has to be because the idea of beauty is defined by my culture, which prizes youth over age.

Helen Garner, an Australian novelist, wrote a powerful essay that highlights this, punchily entitled 'The Insults of Age'. She notes how 'Your face is lined, and your hair is grey, so they think you are weak, deaf, helpless, ignorant and stupid.' While there are more older women in the public eye of late, their remarkable looks are commented upon as being *despite* their years.

I didn't see Susan for a few weeks after her party. Graham had taken her away for their first long holiday in many years. When she returned, I was excited to catch up with her news, and to hear her anecdotes in the usual colourful detail with which she described her day-to-day life. I desperately wanted to hear that she had been able to enjoy her party rather than worrying about her guests, and that she had at least begun to come to terms with the age it marked.

I immediately noticed – and was relieved – that she was empty-handed when I welcomed her back. I was also glad that she didn't apologise for her lack of gift.

'The party was brilliant, Julia! I'm still reeling from it, all these weeks on. Little did I know that my family had other ideas about how I was going to celebrate. You know that I thought I'd booked a venue, sorted the food and music and agonised about the guest list. But on the night, the twins ambushed me. They took me to a different, posher venue, the guest list had clearly been doubled, and there were friends from all over the place – even one who came down from Scotland.

'Graham made a speech and Rob read out something put together by all the kids, and they projected a montage of photos of me through the years. None from my childhood, thank goodness, as I looked so odd back then! But I didn't have to say anything or cut any cake, as agreed. Honestly, it was one of the best nights of my life.'

'That's so good to hear. You deserved every moment. You are much-loved and you make a real difference to many people.'

I was amazed Susan didn't wave my words away or deny them outright – or indeed shudder, as she sometimes did. Instead she took a deep breath and looked at me straight.

'Thank you, Julia. I do know all of that really, but because of our conversations I really tried to savour the kind words said about me, rather than push them away as you have noted I do. I made a point of looking at all the people in the room and reminded myself that they were there because they wanted to be. It was difficult though.'

'I'm sure. I don't think you know how to appreciate yourself without feeling it to be wrong, or indulgent. Or maybe even sinful.'

'I get that more and more now. The kids bought me the most thoughtful gift. I had no idea they knew I wanted to write – they don't know that I'm seeing you. But they clubbed together and signed me up for a creative writing course. It's for complete beginners and they managed to persuade the school to offer me a place without seeing any of my writing. Because it has assignments and deadlines, they thought my fear of letting someone down could give me a kick up the bum. I think they are right.'

'Either that or it's the return of the tyranny of the blank page?'

Susan smiled, remembering the word she had claimed she didn't mean to use when we had first met. In previous conversations I had encouraged her, as she tried to write, to be curious about her thought 'I can't do this' rather than getting up to do something for someone else. This meant making an effort to connect with what she was feeling, and this had become easier over time.

'I think I was on to something after all when I said tyranny. It *was* pretty oppressive growing up and I think I may be frightened that my writing might be judged dimly, and in turn that I might be judged dimly. It's okay to make up stories to tell the kids, though, which seems strange.'

'But your kids and grandkids aren't threatening judges. Maybe there's a significant difference between an unknown reader and them, and also between a story that comes from a private desire to tell it rather than to entertain others. You risk exposing yourself to some pretty harsh scrutiny – your habitual, and hidden, critic has much more to lay into.'

Susan stopped smiling as she took my ideas on board. As magnetic as they were, her smiles often served to deflect attention away from herself. She left with a renewed intention to commit to her first writing assignment for the course, and set herself a task of achieving it by the next time we met.

Susan's course allowed her to push past her strong sense of duty towards other people, and at our next meeting, our final session together, she proudly showed up with her first assignment done: a short story following the theme of freedom. She read it out to me, having already sent it off to her course tutor. As I listened to her read, I privately celebrated her unusual confidence at taking up the space between us.

The story was about a woman who planned to redecorate her house after the last of her children had left home.

She loved to be creative and to make things, but her career and family obligations had got in the way of her desires and passions. While searching in a local charity shop for some clothes she could wear to do the redecorating, she spotted a familiar-looking wedding dress. It was remarkably similar to her own wedding dress, which she had lost in a house move years before.

Intrigued by the similarity, she tried it on and found it fitted well. On closer inspection, she realised that it was in fact her own wedding dress – she remembered the name on the label, and the unusual colour of the lining. She took it home and dyed it a dark blue, and then embellished it with colourful sequins, buttons and feathers. Knowing she had no intention of wearing it publicly, she felt free to be ridiculous.

When she could add no more to it, the woman tried the dress on and immediately noticed how different she felt: confident, clear-headed and energetic. She had an overwhelming urge to sit in front of her laptop and begin the novel she had been thinking about for years. She sat down in her finery and let the words pour out. When tiredness eventually hit in the early hours, she carefully folded up the dress and tucked it under her desk.

Every evening, after an exhausting day of painting and stripping, the woman changed into her dress before sitting down to write again, supercharged with a strange creative force. After a few times of doing this, she noticed some of the feathers and sequins had fallen onto the floor at her feet. She gathered them up and left them on her desk beside her.

The following evening, she scooped up another handful of beautiful debris, and again the evening after that. Over the course of a few weeks the woman's dress became entirely un-embellished, apart from tiny tufts of dark blue thread that had held the adornments in place. But the woman was so consumed with her writing that she barely noticed the growing pile of haberdashery, nor that she was, eventually, sitting in a simple dark blue dress. Consumed with the will to finish her novel, she sat down at her desk one last time, the naked dress at her feet. She didn't even realise that she hadn't put it on.

When Susan finished reading, she placed her tablet on her lap, and her reading glasses on her head. She looked at me with her beautiful smile, clearly delighted to have written something down.

'I can't help but think of your story as reflecting your own experience. You don't need anything to write but your own belief in yourself. Nor do you need to embellish yourself with good deeds to shore up your sense of self-worth. I hope this story represents a new freedom for your mind – without criticism.'

We spoke about her next assignment, and I was encouraged by Susan's conviction as she fleshed out her idea. She was giving herself permission to indulge in her desires, and it seemed that some of her bountiful compassion was returning her way. When we parted for the last time, she pipped me to the post and asked if it was okay to give me a hug. It was easy for me to say yes.

Further Thinking

(Self-criticism is): 'an intense and persistent relationship with the self, characterised by (1) an uncompromising demand for high standards in performance; and (2) an expression of hostility and derogation towards the self when these high standards are – inevitably – not met.'

GOLAN SHAHAR,
Erosion

Do you really deserve to be treated any differently from how you treat others? I don't believe you do. I hope my stories have helped you work out if you give yourself an unnecessarily hard time, and if so, how your self-critic operates to make you do this. Like Charlotte, it may cause you to doubt the worth of your opinions; like Daniel, it might prevent you from forging intimate relationships; like Susan, it might make you avoid taking creative risks; or like Jason it might saturate you in such shame that you end up living a lie. Left to run wild, a self-critic can even make us feel that life is not worth living at all.

Sometimes I meet someone who is able to mitigate their

self-sabotaging habits after discovering their well-hidden self-critic. In other words, simply identifying and labelling it can allow them to ignore it when they need to. But more usually, I find that this awareness can only light the way, leaving much more to be done in order to avoid being negatively affected, or even sabotaged by it. So here I suggest some authors who have helped me, and many of my clients, quieten their self-critic, along with some professional texts for those who are interested in clinical thinking in psychotherapy. I also think that a psychotherapist can help too – but more of that before I reach the end.

Professor Paul Gilbert's *The Compassionate Mind* is an excellent book to begin with, along with *Mindful Compassion* which he co-wrote with a Buddhist monk, Chodron. He has spent decades thinking about self-criticism, and as an evolutionary biologist he brilliantly explains why the human brain is predisposed to it, as well as offering a structured route out of it using the attributes and skills of compassion. Compassion comes up *a lot* in all the works I recommend, as it is the best antidote available to us for self-criticism, and indeed so much else that is wrong with our world.

Among researchers of emotion, compassion describes the feeling we have when we face another's suffering and feel motivated to relieve it. In other words, unlike allied notions of empathy, sympathy, love or altruism, with compassion there's an inner call to action and a conscious turn towards doing it. Gilbert, and the other authors I recommend, teaches us how to do it and pioneered the practice of one of the latest iterations of cognitive behavioural therapy: compassion focused therapy, which is offered by some NHS trusts and a growing number of specialist private practitioners.

Rick Hanson, a US psychologist, treads similar ground to Gilbert. His book *Hardwiring Happiness* is a good place to start, along with his weekly newsletters (you can sign up on rickhanson.net, where you'll find his podcasts too). Like Gilbert, he describes how the evolution of our brains means we tilt towards negativity and self-criticism, coining the memorable phrase 'Velcro for the bad, Teflon for the good'. He emphasises compassionate approaches as a way to soften this hardwiring, drawing on the wisdom traditions of Buddhism in particular.

Dr Kristin Neff, an associate professor at the University of Texas, is a leading researcher in the realm of self-criticism and she sets out the mechanisms and possible reasons for this habit, along with her evidence-based steps to tackle it, in *Self-Compassion*. Her latest book, *Fierce Compassion*, develops her ideas further in the context of misogyny, calling upon women to use their innate strengths to look after themselves and push back. Together with the psychologist Christopher Germer, she has devised an eight-week course to develop self-compassion (mindfulselfcompassionuk.com) and their *Self-Compassion Workbook* is a very useful introduction to the practices that can 'warm our inner climate up' (to steal a metaphor used by them).

The 'compassion work' these authors suggest involves a foundational practice of mindfulness meditation. The American emeritus professor of medicine John Kabat-Zinn is best known for introducing mindfulness into psychological treatments, and his *Full Catastrophe Living* is a seminal and foundational read.

While the other books I mention walk you through medi-tation practices, I always recommend starting with one of the first popular how-to books on the market: *Mindfulness: Finding Peace in a Frantic World* by Dr Danny Penman and Professor Mark Williams. Taught eight-week courses in mindfulness are increasingly easy to find in the UK too, such as by the wise and delightful Ed Halliwell who teaches in Sussex, London and online.

As a psychotherapist, I would be remiss if I didn't mention important texts from key thinkers in my field. They tend to be more interested in formulating a person's self-criticism than in offering practical steps for tackling it to a reader. While they may well be read more by therapists, you may find their ideas resonate with you. Freud is, as ever, a good place to start. In *Mourning and Melancholia* (1917), he described the trait of self-criticism in his depressed (melancholic) patients, noting a 'lowering of the self-regarding feelings to a degree that finds utterance in self-reproaches and self-reviling, and culminates in a delusional expectation of punishment'. Later, in *The Ego and the Id* (1923), he wrote about the superego, a term I often hear from those who *are* aware of their self-critical force. In Freud's now familiar schema, superego refers to one of the three facets of our mind, working alongside our ego and id. While the id refers to our potentially wild and disorganised instinctual desires, our ego is the more organised and conscious 'I' that mediates between the unruly id and the judgemental superego. Our superego develops as a result of our absorbing parental and wider cultural messaging about what is right and wrong, or good and bad, and becomes very harsh for a lot of us. It has, among many of my clients at least, become synonymous with a self-critic.

Karen Horney, a feminist psychoanalyst working at the same time as Freud, echoed these thoughts in *Neurosis and*

Human Growth: The Struggle toward Self-Realization (1950) with her vivid description of a 'tyranny of shoulds' ruling those of us who feel we don't live up to our ideal self and which make us feel deeply flawed, and even self-despising. Albert Ellis, one of the pioneers of cognitive behavioural therapy, also emphasised our tendency to believe in too many shoulds, with his memorable warning against 'musterbation' as a source of self-reproach. He wrote, or co-wrote, seventy-five books and his 1988 *How to Stubbornly Refuse to Make Yourself Miserable about Anything – yes Anything!* is a fantastically lively read.

The charismatic founder of Gestalt therapy, Fritz Perls, comes to life in *Gestalt Therapy Verbatim* (1969). He coined the phrase topdog vs underdog to describe the dynamic that operates between bully and victim, and noted how much that operates within our selves too. If you want a more academic (and therefore denser) read about the pathology of self-criticism, with its inextricable link to depression and other disorders, Sidney Blatt's *Experiences of Depression: Theoretical, Clinical and Research Perspectives* was influential, and built upon by Golan Shahar's extensive *Erosion: The Psychopathology of Self-Criticism* (2015).

If your self-critic is limiting your life or causes you to not function well, please consider supporting your reading, and thinking, with the help of a mental health professional. Acute self-criticism is often bound up with treatable mental health issues, such as stress, depression, addictions or, as mine was, anxiety. It's also a good idea to seek professional support alongside any self-enquiry if it causes you to square up to a traumatic or particularly painful past.

A counselling psychologist, counsellor or psychotherapist

(the last tends to work longer term) could be of help. Your GP may be able to refer you to a local service, but if you – or your employer – are able to fund it privately (and sadly, this tends to mean quicker treatment), my professional organisation, the UK Council for Psychotherapy, lists trusted colleagues on their website, as does the website of the British Association of Counselling and Psychotherapy. You may also want to work with a specialist trained compassionate focused therapist (cft-therapist.com) if Paul Gilbert's work feels to be right for you.

I wouldn't do the job that I do if I wasn't hopeful that a self-critic can be safely put to one side. I think we have the capacity to learn to relate to ourselves in more constructive ways than critical ones, and in so doing we can practise treating ourselves with the care, the kindness and the under-standing that we find so easy to offer others. Many of my clients learnt to do so, and I did too: I got to know how my self-critic behaves, and to understand why she does what she does. She is nowhere near as brutal as she was that winter's day when she convinced me I was so terrible that I needed to be under state surveillance. Instead, she now steps in when it's useful, and leaves me feeling okay. I'm hopeful yours can do the same.

References

Page 1   Penelope Mortimer, *The Pumpkin Eater* (London: Hutchinson, 1962)

Page 5   Tara Brach, *Radical Compassion: Learning to Love Yourself and Your World with the Practice of RAIN* (London: Penguin Life, 2020)

Page 7   Will Storr, *Selfie: How the West Became Self-Obsessed* (London: Picador, 2017)

Page 11   Adam Phillips, 'Against Self-Criticism', *London Review of Books*, 37:5 (5 March 2015)

Page 61   Jia Tolentino, *Trick Mirror: Reflections on Self-Delusion* (London: 4th Estate, 2019)

Page 102   Michael Rosen, *We're Going on a Bear Hunt* (London: Walker, 1989)

Page 111   Audre Lord, 'Eye to Eye: Black Women, Hatred, and Anger', in *Sister Outsider: Essays and Speeches* (Berkeley: Crossing Press, 1984)

Page 116   Reni Eddo-Lodge, *Why I'm No Longer Talking to White People About Race* (London: Bloomsbury, 2017)

Page 120   Simone de Beauvoir (trans. and ed. H. M. Parshley), *The Second Sex* (London: New English Library, 1969)

Page 131   Kristin Neff, 'Why Women Need Fierce Self-Compassion', https://self-compassion.org/women-fierce-self-compassion/

Page 132   Taffy Brodesser-Akner, *Fleishman is in Trouble* (London: Wildfire, 2019)

Page 135   Élisabeth Badinter (trans. Adriana Hunter), *The Conflict: How Modern Motherhood Undermines the Status of Women* (New York: Metropolitan Books, 2012)

Page 147   Joan Didion, *The Year of Magical Thinking* (New York: Knopf, 2005)

Page 148 Emilie Pine, 'From the Baby Years', in *Notes to Self: Essays* (Dublin: Tramp Press, 2018)

Page 152 Adrienne Rich, 'Motherhood in Bondage', *New York Times*, 20 November 1976

Page 156 Badinter (trans. Hunter), *The Conflict*

Page 159 Julia Cameron, *The Artist's Way: A Spiritual Path to Higher Creativity* (London: Souvenir Press, 1992)

Page 160 Ted Hughes, foreword to Sandy Brownjohn, *What Rhymes with 'Secret'?* (London: Hodder Education, 1982)

Page 174 Tara Westover, *Educated: A Memoir* (New York: Random House, 2018)

Page 180 Helen Garner, 'The Insults of Age', *The Monthly*, May 2015

Page 185 Golan Shahar, *Erosion: The Psychopathology of Self-Criticism* (New York: Oxford University Press, 2015)

Acknowledgements

My thanks to my agent Carrie Plitt for her guidance away from ideas without legs and towards one with them, and to my editor Sarah Savitt for believing in me again, and paying such close attention to my drafts. Thanks to my copy-editor Zoe Gullen who faced many mixed, and strangled, metaphors. My friends Pippa Davies, Jane Edwards, Anya Sizer, Afra Turner and Kate O'Brien were very kind to read, and respond to, early inchoate drafts.

My job is a privilege, and I don't think any of my clients would know how much I learn from them and how grateful I am for that. My lengthy – and first – conversation with Professor Paul Gilbert, over a decade ago, inspired me to practise new, and far kinder, ways of responding to the vagaries of my inner world. Along with my subsequent training with Kristin Neff and Christopher Germer, I have found life easier since. I owe these teachers a great deal.

But my biggest thanks, as ever, is to David, without whom this book wouldn't have happened.

Julia Bueno practises full-time as a psychotherapist in London. Her first book, *The Brink of Being: Talking about Miscarriage*, won the British Medical Association Popular Medicine Book Award and was the runner-up for the British Psychological Society Book Award 2021.

She has a particular expertise in working with women, and men, who have experienced a loss in pregnancy or a struggle to conceive. Her writing has been published in *The Times*, the *Sunday Times* and the *New York Times*, and she regularly reviews for the *Times Literary Supplement*.